EDUCATIONAL VIEWS OF BENJAMIN FRANKLIN

AMS PRESS
NEW YORK

BENJAMIN FRANKLIN

(*Frontispiece*)

EDUCATIONAL VIEWS OF BENJAMIN FRANKLIN

Edited By

THOMAS WOODY

Author of

Quaker Education in the Colony and State of New Jersey
A History of Women's Education in the United States
Fürstenschulen in Germany after the Reformation
Early Quaker Education in Pennsylvania

McGRAW-HILL BOOK COMPANY, INC.

NEW YORK AND LONDON

1931

Reprinted from the edition of 1931, New York

First AMS EDITION published 1971

Manufactured in the United States of America

International Standard Book Number: 0-404-07028-0

Library of Congress Catalog Number: 72-153873

AMS PRESS INC.
NEW YORK, N.Y.   10003

DEDICATED
TO
MY STUDENTS

I think, with you, that nothing is of more importance for the public weal than to form and train up youth in wisdom and virtue. Wise and good men are, in my opinion, the strength of a state much more so than riches or arms, which, under the management of ignorance and wickedness, often draw on destruction, instead of providing for the safety of the people. And though the culture bestowed on many should be successful only with a few, yet the influence of those few, and the service in their power, may be very great. Even a single woman, that was wise, by her wisdom saved the city.

I think, also, that general virtue is more probably to be expected and obtained from the education of youth than from the exhortation of adult persons; bad habits and vices of the mind being, like diseases of the body, more easily prevented than cured. I think, moreover, that talents for the education of youth are the gift of God; and that he on whom they are bestowed, whenever a way is opened for the use of them, is as strongly called as if he heard a voice from heaven; nothing more surely pointing out duty, in a public service, than ability and opportunity of performing it.

—Franklin.

PREFACE

Has there ever been an American whose name has appealed to his fellows as powerfully as Franklin's? Washington's youth, as generally presented to them, was too good to believe, much less to imitate. Adams, Jefferson, and the rest were a little too puritanical or aristocratic to make a universal appeal as did Franklin, whose boyhood was often as poverty stricken as their own and yet filled with marvelous adventures. His bourgeois liberalism, achievements in science, and brilliant political successes each left its mark on America and brought her out in the society of nations. These characteristic attainments appealed to mature minds; but to youth he has also been imperfect enough to be human and inspiring. Washington's legendary exploits with a hatchet, oft related, left one cold; but young Franklin, drawing himself with a kite across a pond, running away to New York and Philadelphia, and swimming from Chelsea to Blackfryar's before admiring friends, kindled warm

PREFACE

sympathy and stirred the imagination. And this boy grew up and did great things—apparently with perfect ease. Shall I ever forget the fervor with which I conned and delivered these four lines of my patriotic "piece," on a certain Friday afternoon?

*Ben Franklin flew his kite so high
That he drew the lightning from the sky!
And it didn't come down till the Fourth of July
In Fourteen-ninety-two.*

His great fame and intensely human character have won him numerous biographers—more, perhaps, than any other American. All of them have done him honor, but no one too much. His weakness for wine and women, generally dealt with by recent biographers, if occasionally suppressed by earlier ones, has failed to diminish his glory. Men are inclined to love those who triumph over, or in spite of, weakness. Franklin, the "water American," of whom his English fellow workers made sport, was stronger after he paid the *bien venu* (five shillings for drink) required of all new workmen than before; and was able to wean "a great part of them . . ." from their ". . . muddling breakfast of beer, and bread, and cheese. . . ." Temperate, Franklin was; but never abstentious or puritanical.

The preparation of this small volume on the *Educational Views of Benjamin Franklin* has been facilitated by the labors of numerous Franklin students, the proximity of certain original materials at the University of Pennsylvania, and the kind assistance of Mr. Asa Don Dickinson, librarian of the University of Pennsylvania. To him and to them I express grateful appreciation. It would be supererogatory to list the numerous works consulted; but one may with propriety mention a few of the most useful, even though some excellent titles must be omitted. Among the unusually readable, but not entirely reliable, is the *Life and Times of Benjamin Franklin,* by James Parton, in two volumes (Boston, 1864). More recent and valuable are Paul Leicester Ford's *The Many-sided Franklin* (The Century Company, New York, 1899); Sydney G. Fisher's *The True Benjamin Franklin* (J. B. Lippincott Company, Philadelphia, 1899); and William C. Bruce's *Benjamin Franklin Self-revealed,* in two volumes (G. P. Putnam's Sons, New York, 1917). Two biographies of recent days, Russell Phillips' *Benjamin Franklin, The First*

PREFACE

Civilized American (Brentano, New York, 1926) and Bernard Faÿ's *Franklin The Apostle of Modern Times* (Little, Brown, and Company, Boston, 1929) are readable, living, human, full-length portraits of the man and may be recommended for pleasant as well as profitable reading.

Of greatest value are the attempts that have been made to collect and publish the complete works of Franklin, although, after each editor has completed his work, something new has come to light. Use has been made of *The Works of Benjamin Franklin* ... by Jared Sparks, in ten volumes (Boston, 1836–1840); John Bigelow's *The Works of Benjamin Franklin,* in twelve volumes (G. P. Putnam's Sons, New York, 1904); *The Sayings of Poor Richard,* edited by Paul Leicester Ford (Brooklyn, 1890); and Albert H. Smyth's *The Writings of Benjamin Franklin,* in ten volumes (The Macmillan Company, New York, 1905–1907). To the publishers the author wishes to express his appreciation of their graciously given permission to make quotations. Bibliographical information, concerning other sources quoted, is given in the appropriate places in the text.

PREFACE

Among bibliographical aids, the *List of Benjamin Franklin Papers,* in the Library of Congress, compiled by W. C. Ford (Government Printing Office, Washington, 1905), the *Franklin Bibliography* by Paul Leicester Ford (Brooklyn, 1889), and the *Calendar of the Papers of Benjamin Franklin,* in the Library of the American Philosophical Society, edited by I. M. Hays, in five volumes (American Philosophical Society, Philadelphia, 1908), have been most useful.

In calling the roll of famous American educators many probably will occur before the name of Franklin. The reasons for this seem to lie in the fact that he was not much given to theorizing, spoken or written, about what education should be, but gave his efforts in support of practical undertakings of the broadest educational import. To encourage these he occasionally prepared plans, proposals, projects. The profound influence exerted by his essays on American education, in the narrower, as well as in the broader, sense places Franklin among the greatest American educators—which is by way of saying that the greatest educators are frequently not professional ones. Our usual, narrow definition of education and Franklin's dazzling career in politics,

PREFACE

called by Horace Mann the "god of Americans," have also served to diminish the attention given him as an educator.

In this text modern spelling and capitalization have been employed, though, considering the tenderness Mr. Franklin felt for his capitals (he criticised sharply the work of printers who thought to improve the appearance of the text by suppressing them), it is perhaps an unkind thing to do. It is futile, however, for every present student of education to trip his toes on superfluous capitals when his real business is to obtain an understanding of Franklin's ideas.

The writer wishes to express his thanks to Dr. E. H. Reisner, of Teachers College, Columbia University, for assistance and courtesies; and to W. L. Woody, for aid in preparing the manuscript and seeing it through the press.

T. W.

UNIVERSITY OF PENNSYLVANIA,
February, 1931.

CONTENTS

	PAGE
PREFACE	ix

CHAPTER I

A Sketch of Franklin's Life 1

CHAPTER II

Methods and Agencies of Self-Education 37
  Rules for a Club Established for Mutual Improvement . 47
  A Proposal for Promoting Useful Knowledge among the British Plantations in America 58
  Advice to a Young Tradesman 64
  The Way to Wealth 67
  Plan of Moral Education and Self-examination . . . 85
  Rules of Health and Long Life 99

CHAPTER III

First Steps of a Practical Education 101
  A Letter on the Temple of Learning 103
  Idea of the English School 120
  Of the Education of Girls 130
  A Petition of the Left Hand to Those Who Have the Superintendency of Education 134

CONTENTS

CHAPTER IV

PAGE

FRANKLIN AND THE ACADEMY 137

   Proposals Relating to the Education of Youth in Pennsylvania 149

   Constitutions of the Public Academy in the City of Philadelphia 182

   Observations Relative to the Intentions of the Original Founders of the Academy in Philadelphia 192

   On the Usefulness of the Mathematics 229

CHAPTER V

EDUCATION OF ORPHANS AND NEGROES 235

   Hints for Consideration Respecting the Orphan Schoolhouse in Philadelphia 237

   On the Slave-trade 240

   An Address to the Public from the Pennsylvania Society for Promoting the Abolition of Slavery 248

   Plan for Improving the Condition of the Free Blacks . . 250

INDEX 255

CHAPTER I

A SKETCH OF FRANKLIN'S LIFE

I

BENJAMIN FRANKLIN, the fifteenth of seventeen children, was born in Boston, Jan. 6 (O. S.), 1706, to Josiah and Abiah (Folger) Franklin. Of the latter, the daughter of Peter Folger, "a godly, learned Englishman," he wrote in his *Autobiography* that she was possessed of "an excellent constitution" and never had any sickness till that of which she died. In like vein he spoke of his father. Both lived "lovingly together" for fifty-five years and, "by constant labor and industry," brought up their large family. In the eyes of the son, "He was a pious and prudent man; she, a discreet and virtuous woman."

In this family, maintained by such labor and industry, young Benjamin had a training in simplicity and frugality that marked his life. More was thought of what entered the head than of what entered the stomach; and, as he later asserted, "To this day if I am asked I

FRANKLIN'S EDUCATIONAL VIEWS

can scarcely tell a few hours after dinner what I dined upon."

Franklin was born of old English Protestant stock which for three centuries had lived in the village of Ecton, in Northamptonshire. He was the youngest son of the youngest son for five generations back. All who are wont to marvel at Franklin's zeal in searching all things and his caustic thrusts at the shams of ecclesiastics may find antecedents of this alertness and religious interest in the anecdote of his grandfather, who got hold of an English Bible at a time when it was dangerous to possess one and secured it by hiding it "within the cover of a joint-stool." While he read it, "one of the children stood at the door to give notice if he saw the apparitor coming, who was an officer of the spiritual court."[1] Franklin's non-conforming tendencies had then a strong precedent on his father's side. From his maternal grandfather, possibly to a greater extent, he inherited a liberality which extended even to Baptists and Quakers. In the latter, and in his Uncle Benjamin as well, the lad had prototypes for the love of verse

[1] *The Life of Benjamin Franklin, Written by Himself*, p. 13, New York, 1856.

A SKETCH OF FRANKLIN'S LIFE

making, which he cultivated as a part of his self-education.

Franklin's forebears had been men of practical industry, being regularly trained up in some "art or mystery" by the apprenticeship method, as was the custom and the law of England. The eldest sons, from generation to generation, had been blacksmiths. His father and two uncles, Benjamin and John, served an apprenticeship in dyeing, while his Uncle Thomas was bred a blacksmith, according to family tradition. But, though bred a smith, he turned scrivener and became a prominent man and "a chief mover of all public-spirited undertakings for the county or town of Northampton, and his own village. . . ."

All Franklin's elder brothers were put out as apprentices to certain trades; but upon Ben, the tithe of his father's sons, the dove descended. He had given early signs of budding talents which had led friends of the family to think he would make a good scholar. He said, himself, later in life, that he could not remember when he could not read. According to the then prevailing tradition that bright boys become ministers, he was put, at eight years of age, to the grammar school, the first rung of the ladder leading to the highest science, sacred theology. His Uncle Benjamin was heartily pleased with this direction of his promising nephew and offered to give him volumes of sermons, in his home-made shorthand, with which to set up shop.

Franklin, late in life, wrote a little essay on a boyhood experience, the philosophic lesson of which was "don't pay too much for a whistle." His father seems to have known this philosophy thoroughly before him. At any rate, in "view of the expense of a college education . . . and the mean living many so educated were afterwards able to obtain . . ." he withdrew Ben from grammar school within the year, though the lad had made great progress, and put him to study arithmetic and writing, under George Brownell. Under this far-famed master, Franklin learned "fair writing" but "bilged" in arithmetic, which he later mastered by himself by working through the renowned book of Cocker.

At the age of ten, Franklin was taken home to assist in the father's business, that of "sope-boiler" and tallow chandler, which he had taken up when he could not support the family by dyeing. So hearty was the boy's dislike of it, however, his father feared he might run

A SKETCH OF FRANKLIN'S LIFE

away and accordingly sought, by visiting many occupations, to select one for which Benjamin was suited. This instruction through observation proved of great value to the boy, and, at length, in his thirteenth year, he was sent to his cousin, a cutler, "on liking." The cousin expected a fee, however, and, this displeasing Ben's father, he was again removed.

Something had to be done. Little Ben, like most boys who live near harbors, wanted to go to sea. Hatred of cutting wicks, filling moulds, boiling soap, and running errands intensified his longing for the freedom of life on the deep. His father was determined to forestall this fulfillment of desire; but, in spite of it, the boy managed to spend much time in the water, learned to be an expert swimmer and to handle boats.

The farther quest for an apprenticeship, more agreeable to the youth's aptitude, seems to have been guided by his obvious bookish inclination. He was, from early childhood, a great reader and spent all he could get hold of for books. In his father's small collection, he found chiefly the stones of polemic divinity. When he tells us that he read most of them, we should not be surprised, for it was customary in that century for children to cut their spiritual teeth on solid matter. Whether he knew the dour pages of the *Old Bay Psalm Book* and Wigglesworth's *Day of Doom,* we are not told; nor did he mention the titles in "polemic divinity" which he strove to digest. But we do know he lamented, later in life, that ". . . at a time when I had such a thirst for knowledge, more proper books had not fallen in my way . . ." If, however, most of the literature that fell in his way was unpalatable and indigestible stuff, it is undoubtedly true that the serious nature of all of it and the substantial value of some classic portions directed his mind into those deep and serious channels which touched so many sides of human life. Franklin himself reports that he was pleased with *Pilgrim's Progress* and bought a collection of Bunyan's works. He soon parted with them, however, and purchased R. Burton's *Historical Collections* the world realities and mysteries of which seem to have profited him more.

More pleasing, more formative in their influence, and of far more lasting worth, if we may abide by his judgment at the age of sixty-five, were Plutarch's *Lives* in which he "read abundantly," Defoe's *Essays on Projects,* the *Spectator,* with which he made acquaintance through an odd volume, a book by Tryon—*The Way to Health, Long Life and Happiness, or a Discourse of Temperance*—and, a little later, Locke's *Conduct of the Understanding* and the *Art of Thinking,* by the Gentlemen of Port Royal. A book most often referred to as influencing the trend of his life was Mather's *Bonifacius, An Essay upon the Good that is to be Devised and Designed by those who desire to Answer the Great End of Life, and to do Good while they live* . . . His first literary efforts, published in the *New England Courant,* appeared under the modest pseudonym, Silence Dogood. In 1784, completing a period of brilliant service to the colonies and youthful states abroad, he wrote ". . . If I have been, as you seem to think, a useful citizen, the public owes the advantage of it to that book." Due to it, ". . . I have always set a greater value on the character of a doer of good, than on any other kind of reputation . . ."[2] The *Memorabilia* of Xenophon and the writings of Collins and Shaftesbury also influenced his thought, as far as religion was concerned. To the latter two, especially, he was indebted for deistical tendencies

[2] From SMYTH, A. H., *The Writings of Benjamin Franklin,* Vol. IX, p. 208. (By permission of The Macmillan Company, publishers, New York, 1905.)

which were greatly stimulated by later contacts in France and England.

With such a turn for books, the most promising apprenticeship open to him, if he were not to be prepared for the ministry, was that of printing. To his brother James, who had just brought equipment from London for setting up a shop, he was therefore apprenticed at the age of twelve, to serve until he should be twenty. In this environment, his appetite for reading and the means to satisfy it increased. He began to write ballads, some of which were printed and sold about the streets. Among the best of these was "The Light-house Tragedy," which attracted considerable favorable attention.

In 1721, James Franklin began publication of the *New England Courant*. Benjamin helped distribute it to customers and ere long plucked up courage to try his hand —unknown to others—at writing an article. Under the unobtrusive *nom de plume,* Silence Dogood, he introduced himself, at the age of sixteen, as the widow of a rural preacher and proceeded, after preliminary bows and polite formalities, to criticize the privileged classes, the clergy, the collegians, the government, after the fashion of certain London papers of the day and also in keeping with the spirit of other contributors to the *Courant*. Fourteen papers appeared during the summer of 1722. In the second of them, the writer closed with an account of his own character. It may not be amiss to quote this paragraph, indicating at the very beginning of his career as author how firmly Franklin was attached to certain principles which he never forsook throughout life.

"I shall conclude this with my own character, which (one would think) I should be best able to give. Know then, that I am an enemy to vice, and a friend to virtue. I am one of an extensive charity, and a great forgiver of private injuries: A hearty lover of the clergy and all good men, and a mortal enemy to arbitrary government and unlimited power. I am naturally very jealous for the rights and liberties of my country: And the least appearance of an encroachment on those invaluable privileges, is apt to make my blood boil exceedingly. I have likewise a natural inclination to observe and reprove the faults of others, at which I have an excellent faculty. I speak of this by way of warning to all such whose offences shall come under my cognizance, for I never intend to wrap my talent in a napkin." [3]

[3] *Ibid.*, Vol. II, p. 7. (By permission of The Macmillan Company, publishers, New York, 1905.)

One of his most pointed letters was an attack upon the collegiate education of the day.[4]

It was but a short time until James Franklin was haled into court because numerous attacks had gravely offended members of the assembly. He was put into prison and ordered to discontinue publication of the *Courant,* and it was decided that Benjamin should be given charge of it. As the publicly acknowledged head of the paper, at seventeen years of age, Benjamin could not, of course, continue in the compromising position of apprentice. His papers therefore were destroyed, but he signed others secretly which promised his brother his services. When the latter was released and returned to the shop, the life of Benjamin was again darkened. His brother had always been of a mean temper, overbearing, and had even beaten him. On his return, these tactics were resumed. Being now legally free from his service, Benjamin refused to tolerate his brother's insolence longer and left the shop.

II

Finding he could secure no work with other printers

[4] See pp. 103–109.

A SKETCH OF FRANKLIN'S LIFE

in the city, as James had warned all against him, he sold some of his books and secretly secured passage on a sloop to New York. There he inquired for employment at the print shop of William Bradford, who, having no work to offer, advised him to continue to Philadelphia where his son, Andrew Bradford, publisher of the *Weekly Mercury,* had just lost his assistant, Aquila Rose. After passing four days, he left New York, taking a boat to Amboy and thence on foot to Burlington, whence he was able to secure a boat to Philadelphia.

Hungry, much stained by foot travel—it had rained steadily as he trudged across the flats of New Jersey—with only a Dutch dollar and some coppers in his pocket, he landed at Market Street Wharf in Philadelphia. After giving the coppers to the boatman for passage (he assures us men will often give much through fear of being thought to have little), he began to inspect the streets of his future home. His pockets were bulging with extra shirts and stockings, and, because of his generally bedraggled appearance, he feared he might be taken as a runaway servant, such as he had often seen advertised on the back page of his brother's paper. In fact, a little way back, in New Jersey, some one had questioned him suspiciously. But Benjamin was too practical to waste much time in wondering. Having found his way to a bakeshop, he continued with more satisfaction (for the bread cost only a threepence) his walk around the city. Coming to the Quaker meeting house, he entered and sat down; as all were waiting for the spirit to move them, he went to sleep and was awakened only as the meeting broke up by a Friend who was going out. On the street, some one directed him to the "Crooked Billet" where he supped and spent the whole night in refreshing slumber.

Efforts to secure a desirable printer's job were only a little more successful here than elsewhere. Bradford had no permanent work for him, so he accepted a place at Keimer's and began to think that he might after a while become an independent printer, especially as neither Keimer nor Bradford impressed him as being able to meet the needs of the rising city. Not long after, Governor Keith began to take an interest in him and caused him to think his dream might come true. At the latter's suggestion he soon returned to his father, with a letter from Keith, urging him to furnish money to set up the new printing office. The father was cordially glad to see Benjamin return, obviously prosperous, but equally cautious about advancing money. The best Benjamin got was a promise of help at the age of twenty-two, if, in the meantime, he were able to gather most of the funds himself. Returning to Philadelphia, he was surprised by Keith's offer to do what his father had refused. "But," said Keith, "go yourself to London to select equipment," and promised to give letters of introduction and credit. Franklin, elated, made ready for departure and said farewell to Deborah Read, whom he was to have married. When the boat set sail, however, the letters not being ready, Keith bade him cordial farewell and said he would receive the letters on reaching London. Arriving there, he finally realized the emptiness of Keith's promises—for there were no letters for him on the packet—and set about to "find himself" in a strange city.

The experience in London developed Franklin. He found work at Palmer's famous print shop for a year and then finished out his sojourn of eighteen months at the printery of Watts. Besides this apprenticeship, although he had a fling in the gay world, made a few *errata,* he tells us in the *Autobiography,* and lost much through his indiscreet friend, Ralph, he also gained the more valuable experience of acquaintance with books and with a few prominent learned men, such as Lyons, Mandeville, and Pemberton. These connections, strengthened and multiplied on later visits, were of great consequence throughout his life. It is also to be noted that he was stimulated to do some writing—"A Dissertation on Liberty and Necessity, Pleasure and Pain," suggested by his work in setting up Wollaston's *Religion of Nature Delineated*. He was now nineteen.

Through flattering attention, gained by his prowess in swimming, Franklin was all but persuaded to remain in England as a professional teacher to the sons of Sir William Wyndham, when Mr. Denham, a merchant, agreed to take him back to Philadelphia at a salary of fifty pounds a year.

III

His *Wanderjahre* at an end, Franklin, on reaching Philadelphia (1726), set out to rectify errors. He had, as a result of all labor since leaving Boston, only his experience. He owed money, moreover. But he had

A SKETCH OF FRANKLIN'S LIFE

as support of his public and philanthropic enterprises. Their stock of private books being small, a common pool was made to which all members of the club contributed. Observing, however, that the number of books was never so great as expected and there being some "inconvenience" for "want of due care of them," this method was soon given up and each member "took his books home again." Franklin now undertook to establish a subscription library (1731). A set of proposals were put into writing by Brockden, "our great scrivener," fifty subscribers were obtained at forty shillings, and ten shillings a year for fifty years, and a charter was later obtained.

Franklin looked on it with great pride. It was, of course, "a means of improvement . . ." for himself; more than that, ". . . reading became fashionable; and our people, having no public amusements to divert their attention from study, became better acquainted with books, and in a few years were observed by strangers to be better instructed and more intelligent than people of the same rank generally are in other countries." [5] He

[5] *The Life of Benjamin Franklin, Written by Himself,* p. 87, New York, 1856.

gave much to promote libraries. In 1755, he wrote John Hancock about starting, and himself contributed to, a subscription fund for the Harvard Library.[6] In 1782, a donation was made to the library at Franklin, Mass.

The library at Philadelphia was the first of a long series of institutions Franklin labored to create. In 1743, "A Proposal" was issued "for Promoting Useful Knowledge among the British Plantations in America," which resulted in the American Philosophical Society, of which Franklin was long the secretary and, after 1769, the honored president until the time of his death. Six years later, he published the pamphlet which led to founding the Academy and College, now the University of Pennsylvania. Franklin's thought on education and the example of the new College in Philadelphia had a profound influence on some of the men concerned with founding the University of North Carolina, though this leadership lost control later, just as did Franklin's in the University of Pennsylvania.[7] While the Academy

[6] Sept. 11, 1755. A. H. SMYTH, *The Writings of Benjamin Franklin,* Vol. III, pp. 285–286. (The Macmillan Company, New York, 1905.)

[7] DRAKE, W. E., "Benjamin Franklin and the University of North Carolina," *The High School Journal,* Vol. XII, No. 2, pp. 68–76.

A SKETCH OF FRANKLIN'S LIFE

was getting under way (1751), he promoted the organization of the Pennsylvania Hospital, the first of the kind in America. In 1752, he aided in creating the first chartered fire insurance company. Four years later, Franklin was responsible for the introduction of street-cleaning, paving, and lighting in Philadelphia. From this time onward, he was almost exclusively occupied with public political business—so much, indeed, as to leave little opportunity for that philosophic retirement he often desired.

At the time his mind was fixed upon the creation of a society to promote scientific discoveries and the establishment of a school that would teach living rather than dead things, he was also busy with certain scientific improvements. The questions discussed by the Junto, at its very founding, reveal an interest in heating systems. In 1742, he invented the Franklin stove as a substitute for the open fireplace so generally used; and two years later, published an account of it. Then the most challenging interest of all appeared. Electrical phenomena were being discussed in the learned circles of Europe, with more emphasis on theory than demonstration. Franklin's practical genius turned to demonstration. With Kinnersley and other neighbors he studied the ability of metal points to receive and discharge "electrical fire." Musschoenbroek's experiments with the Leyden jars were tested. Franklin happily decided to call the two types of force "positive" and "negative." More important still, experiments of a very simple kind were used to prove that lightning and electrical fire were the same; and application to everyday life was found in the lightning rod, which made Franklin a magician to the whole civilized world. The first experiments had been begun in 1745; in 1747, the theory of electricity, known as the "Franklinian theory," was advanced; and, two years later, the identity of lightning and electricity was demonstrated. In 1751, his *Experiments and Observations on Electricity* appeared in London; and the year following, in translation, at Paris. In 1755, his *New Experiments and Observations on Electricity* . . . was published at London. Three years thereafter, a German translation of his *Electrical Experiments* was brought out in Leipzig. Though credited throughout the world as the originator of the views set forth in these works, it should be noted, in passing, that Franklin has been accused of appropriating the

A SKETCH OF FRANKLIN'S LIFE

discoveries of Ebenezer Kinnersley. H. W. Smith, in the *Life and Correspondence of the Rev. William Smith* (Philadelphia, 1880), stated the case against Franklin. This author, however, wrote as the partizan of Dr. William Smith, between whom and Franklin considerable bitterness had arisen. His obvious bias leaves the author's conclusions, that Kinnersley originated and Franklin copied, open to serious question.

Space will not permit description of Franklin's varied experiences in the rôle of scientist. But to the search for useful knowledge he bent his efforts whenever the affairs of business and politics permitted. With the coming of peace and leisure, in 1783, we find him going to see the ascension of a Montgolfier balloon, with a keen interest in the experiment itself as well as the possible practical uses to which it might be put. "It does not seem to me a good reason," he said, "to decline prosecuting a new experiment which apparently increases the power of a man over matter, till we can see to what use that power may be applied." [8] In 1784, he was one

---

[8] A letter to Sir Joseph Banks. From A. H. SMYTH, *The Writings of Benjamin Franklin,* Vol. IX, p. 117. (By permission of The Macmillan Company, publishers, New York, 1905.)

FRANKLIN'S EDUCATIONAL VIEWS

of a commission, appointed by Louis XVI, which resulted in the exposure of mesmerism.

Returning home, after ten years of exacting public service in France, he occupied most of his time in writing and making observations of the ocean. His eyes were always toward the future. Many friends who had often urged the completion of his *Autobiography* might have thought, had they seen him, that their wish was coming true. Instead, he finished a paper, later presented to the American Philosophical Society, on a question that had engaged the attention of the first meetings of the Junto, "The Causes and Cures of Smoking Chimneys." Three other contributions were made to the Society, in 1785 and 1786—a paper on "Maritime Observations," being the result of labor on many voyages; "A Description of a New Stove for Burning of Pit Coal and Consuming All Its Smoke"; and "A Slowly Sensible Hygrometer."

Pennsylvania politics were as muddied in the eighteenth century as our own. Franklin took part in politics of the city and state, filling many offices though asking for none. His remarkable ability to do things, once it became known, was the lodestone that drew offices

A SKETCH OF FRANKLIN'S LIFE

to him. His many personal friends in the Junto, the Masonic Lodge (of which he became Grand Master in 1734), and other organizations were, at times, strong supports. In 1736, Franklin mentions, he received his "first promotion," being chosen clerk of the General Assembly. The next year he was named postmaster of Philadelphia and became justice of the peace. In 1753, he became deputy postmaster-general, serving till 1774, when he was dismissed by the British Government. In 1747, Franklin was active in establishing means of defense for Philadelphia; and two years later was named, by the Governor, one of the peace commissioners. From 1750 to 1764, he was yearly elected to the Pennsylvania Assembly. More and more his mind dwelt on the importance of a union of the Colonies. The post office, he held, was one of the most important agencies in the promotion of this union. At the Albany Convention (1754) he presented a plan which was accepted, though it failed of approval by the Lords of Trade and the several Colonial assemblies. The years 1755 and 1756 represent the height of his military career. Supplies were obtained through his pledges to the Germans for Braddock's army, and he himself served as colonel of a

FRANKLIN'S EDUCATIONAL VIEWS

Philadelphia regiment against the French and Indians. In 1757, the Pennsylvania Assembly sent Franklin to England to present their petition to the King regarding the taxation of proprietary lands. This mission was at length terminated by a successful compromise. In 1764, he became speaker of the Assembly and successfully promoted the petition to make Pennsylvania a royal province. In the same year, he was sent again to England as the Colony's agent and while there became a most energetic opponent of the Stamp Act, eventually contributing largely to its repeal (1765). He then became, in rapid succession, agent for several American colonies—Georgia (1768), New Jersey (1769), and Massachusetts (1770). During this long service, every effort was made to promote reconciliation and a peaceable adjustment of economic and political differences between England and the Colonies. One of Franklin's favorite schemes was the development of the British empire, with an American parliament subject to the King. All coming to naught and his safety in England really being imperiled, he returned to Philadelphia in 1775, to learn, on arriving, that war had already begun. He was at once named to the Continental Congress,

A SKETCH OF FRANKLIN'S LIFE

served on a committee to draw up the Declaration of Independence, drew up "Articles of Confederation and Perpetual Union," and was made postmaster-general of the Colonies, by act of Congress. After signing the Declaration of Independence, he was unanimously chosen by Congress as one of three ambassadors to France. It is characteristic of Franklin that, before sailing on the *Reprisal,* he collected all his available money and loaned it to Congress.

As the troublous affairs after 1775 began to press more and more upon him, he gave less and less time to philosophical interests. Nothing must impress one more, turning the pages produced by Franklin's pen, than the brusque manner in which the business of war crowded out the affairs of science. One recalls Franklin's words, "There never was a good war or a bad peace." That this was not mere rhetoric is proved by numerous passages in his letters.[9]

In France he became the idol of the day, if not, indeed, of the century. What would have happened to the American cause if it had rested on the diplomacy of a Deane, Lee, or Adams, none of whom seemed to be

[9] *Old South Leaflets,* Vol. VII, No. 162.

able to understand how things were to be done outside Anglo-Saxon circles, is not hard to conjecture. Franklin, fêted by society and honored everywhere for his reputation in philosophy, bided his time and did not hasten negotiations in too orderly a fashion. He was used to the diplomacy of friendliness; a quip, a glass of wine, a song he found useful in personal circles—and in those of diplomacy as well. To a friend he wrote, while in England: "I shall apply this parcel [twelve bottles of American wine] as I did the last towards winning the hearts of the friends of our country . . ." [10] By 1777 he was able to obtain the first gift of two million livres, later supplemented by three million (1778), one million (1779), eight million (1780 and 1781), and six million more in 1782. In 1781, he tendered his resignation to Congress, on account of ill health, but, on request, continued to serve. A preliminary treaty of peace was negotiated with Britain in 1782, the final treaty, recognizing the independence of the United States, being signed in 1783. Other important treaties were made with France, Sweden, and Prussia. After

[10] Feb. 20, 1768. From A. H. SMYTH, *The Writings of Benjamin Franklin,* Vol. V, p. 104. (By permission of The Macmillan Company, publishers, New York, 1905.)

A SKETCH OF FRANKLIN'S LIFE

returning to Philadelphia (1785), his most important political services were performed as president of the Philadelphia City Council, Governor of the state, and member of the Constitutional Convention. In 1787, his continuous interest in a scientific approach to all problems led to an active effort to establish "The Society for Political Enquiries," aiming at the promotion of political science.

His political life was full of stirring deeds. He filled it with stirring words as well. Slogans—propaganda—have now a fine technique and an army to spread them. Franklin was an adept at creation and dissemination in his century. He has been called the first American cartoonist. His clever slogans and epigrams, "Join or die" and "If we do not hang together, we shall all hang separately," are fair samples of his ability to write treatises in single sentences. His biographers agree that he listened much and talked little. As no word was wasted, few were necessary. Franklin voted to adopt the Constitution, even though it did not meet his approval in every way, for, as he put it, ". . . there is no form of government but what may be a blessing to the people, if well administered . . ." He knew that eternal vigi-

FRANKLIN'S EDUCATIONAL VIEWS

lance is the price of liberty. This government, he declared, ". . . can end in despotism, as other forms have done before it, only when the people shall become so corrupted as to need despotic government, being incapable of any other."

Franklin's real honors were his public offices which he filled well and his successes in scientific and philanthropic pursuits. But formal honors and distinctions, also, were showered upon him by his fellow men. His publications on electricity led at once to the award of the Copley Gold Medal by the Royal Society (1753) and the honorary Master of Arts by Harvard and Yale (1753) and by the College of William and Mary (1756). He was, at the same time, elected fellow of the Royal Society and member of the Society for the Encouragement of Arts, Manufactures and Commerce, in London. In 1759, he became honorary member of the Philosophical Society of Edinburgh and received the Doctorate of Laws at the University of St. Andrews. Oxford made him Doctor of Civil Law in 1762, and in 1766 he was chosen a member of the Königliche Gesellschaft der Wissenschaften, at Göttingen. From 1769 till his death he was president of the American Philosophical Society.

A SKETCH OF FRANKLIN'S LIFE

In 1771, he was honored by membership in the Bataafsch Genootschap der Proefondervindelijke Wijsbegeerte at Rotterdam and, in 1772, was one of the eight foreign members in the Royal Academy of Sciences at Paris. His membership in these societies was far from an empty affair. He maintained till his death a lively personal and scientific correspondence in nine languages. And now, in rapid succession, the Royal Medical Society, Paris (1777); the American Academy of Arts and Sciences, Boston (1781); the Academy of Science, Letters and Arts, Padua (1781); the Royal Society of Edinburgh (1783); the Royal Academy of History, Madrid (1784); the Manchester (England) Literary and Philosophical Society; the Société Royale de Physique, d'Histoire Naturelle et des Arts d'Orléans; the Académie des Sciences, Belles Lettres et des Arts, Lyons, all in 1785; the Medical Society of London (1787); and the Imperial Academy of Sciences at St. Petersburg honored him by their fellowship.

Many questions have been raised about Franklin's religion, but the matter ought to be clear. Throughout life, he was an enemy of ecclesiastical form. Though he declared himself a "lover of the clergy," in one of the early Dogood letters, he was a sharp critic. It seems nearer the truth to say he loved some good men whom he found in the ministry—for example, Whitefield. Nevertheless, under the influence of his dissenting father and uncle, he had imbibed a strong interest in religious questions which is evident in much of his writing. He says, himself, I was ". . . religiously educated as a Presbyterian," but the indirect education of everyday life had a profounder influence. In France, he was generally thought a Quaker. Church attendance he found of less profit than reading, though he "had still an opinion of its propriety and of its utility when rightly conducted." Now and then, he said, he was prevailed on to attend the "administrations" of the Presbyterian minister in Philadelphia, "once for five Sundays successively." He regularly supported the church, however. Whitefield, with his oratorical display and theatrical ability, drew Franklin away from his reading; and the Philadelphia printer became his staunchest defender but not his convert. A blue view of life and a blue Sunday made him arch his eyebrows. "I should be glad to know what it is that distinguishes Connecticut religion from common religion . . ." He had just been visiting

A SKETCH OF FRANKLIN'S LIFE

on the Continent and found ". . . plenty of singing, fiddling, and dancing. I looked around for God's judgments, but saw no signs of them . . ."

Franklin's early reading, association with philosophers of the day, and the thought common in Masonic circles encouraged a deistic religious philosophy. His everyday religion was to do good. The attempt to rewrite the Book of Common Prayer had little to do with his fundamental religious belief, though that and other acts affected others' views about it. The members of the Constitutional Convention, who doubtless thought him an atheist, were shocked when he proposed to open the sessions with prayer.

Franklin spoke seldom of his own belief. When he did, he set forth the rôle of religion in the control of conduct. An author, who asked him to read a manuscript, was criticized, for ". . . by the argument it contains against the doctrines of a particular providence . . . you strike at the foundation of all religion . . ." To Ezra Stiles, he wrote, as he was about to die:

"You desire to know something of my religion. It is the first time I have been questioned upon it. But I cannot take your curiosity amiss, and shall endeavor in a few words to gratify it. Here is my creed. I believe in one God, creator of the universe. That he governs it by his providence. That he ought to be worshipped. That the most acceptable service we render to him is doing good to his other children. That the soul of man is immortal, and will be treated with justice in another life respecting its conduct in this. These I take to be the fundamental principles of all sound religion, and I regard them as you do in whatever sect I meet with them.

"As to Jesus of Nazareth, my opinion of whom you particularly desire, I think his system of morals and his religion, as he left them to us, the best the world ever saw or is like to see; but I apprehend it has received various corrupting changes, and I have, with most of the present dissenters in England, some doubts as to his divinity; though it is a question I do not dogmatize upon, having never studied it, and think it needless to busy myself with it now, when I expect soon an opportunity of knowing the truth with less trouble. I see no harm, however, in its being believed, if that belief has the good consequence, as probably it has, of making his doctrines more respected and more observed; especially as I do not perceive, that the Supreme takes it amiss, by distinguishing the unbelievers in his government of the world with any peculiar marks of his displeasure."[11]

After suffering much in the last years and acutely from pleurisy from the first of April, Franklin died Apr. 17, 1790. Assured he would improve, he remarked, "I hope not"; and, when they sought to make him comfortable, he assured them "A dying man can do nothing easy."

Biographers have sought in varied ways to describe Franklin. The complexity of his life and voluminous nature of his contributions test the descriptive powers of language. Many years ago, one wrote ". . . If we can imagine a circumference which shall express humanity, we can place within it no one man who will reach out to approach it, and to touch it, at so many points as will Franklin." By others he has been called the "amazing," and "the many-sided." *The Encyclopædia Britannica* has well pointed out that it is impossible to summarize so versatile a genius. In these few pages the futility of the

[11] BIGELOW, JOHN, *The Works of Benjamin Franklin,* Vol. XII, pp. 185-186. (By permission of G. P. Putnam's Sons, publishers, New York, 1904.)

task will have been evident. It is difficult enough when space is unlimited.

By two of his most recent biographers he has been named "the apostle of modern times" and "the first civilized American." Certainly he earned the former title. If to promote scientific knowledge rather than superstitious guesses and wonderment; if to prefer sound morals to theology; if to advance liberalism and to shun bigotry; if to take a world view when myopic eyes could scarcely see beyond village boundaries; and if to do good to one's fellow men rather than shout "Yea, yea, Lord," are marks of civilization, he fully merited the latter.

CHAPTER II

METHODS AND AGENCIES OF SELF-EDUCATION

Including the "Rules for a Club Established for Mutual Improvement" (1728); "A Proposal for Promoting Useful Knowledge among the British Plantations in America" (1743); "Advice to a Young Tradesman" (1748); "The Way to Wealth" (1757); a "Plan of Moral Education and Self-examination," described in the *Autobiography;* and "Rules of Health and Long Life" (1742).

I

It is a fact of no mean significance that Franklin rose to eminence in numerous fields of human activity. Its importance is enhanced in our minds when we recall that he had less than two years of formal schooling; that all else he attained was through his own endeavors. When a minister to France was to be selected, Franklin was equal to if not better than the rest, though there were many college men in the Congress. French, Italian and Spanish were all pursued in this independent way. While studying Italian, Franklin was urged to play chess with a friend who was also studying the same language. As chess would take so much time from Italian, Franklin agreed to play only on condition that the victor should impose a task in translation or grammar to be completed before their next meeting. Thus they beat each other into a knowledge of that tongue. It must be admitted that self-taught is sometimes badly taught. Thus, though Franklin read French and learned to speak it when in France, he was never quite sure he understood the whole of a conversation and always found writing French letters a great drag on his time. To one friend he apologized for writing in English: "It costs me too much time to write in that language and after all is very bad French."

As a result of having come at a knowledge of languages through his own efforts, Franklin was led to believe in a certain orderly progress from the nearest and easiest to the most remote and difficult—a view common enough to other Realists, before his day. Just as Comenius had provided a vernacular school, from six to twelve, to precede the Latin School, Franklin urged an English School [1] as the first most natural step in formal schooling; and, as Ratke would begin language instruction

[1] See pp. 118–130.

in German, using *Genesis* as a text, Franklin would begin with English and emphasize the use of his old friend the *Spectator* and other classics. His argument follows:

"I have already mentioned that I had only one year's instruction in a Latin School, and that when very young, after which I neglected that language entirely. But, when I had attained an acquaintance with the French, Italian, and Spanish, I was surprised to find, on looking over a Latin Testament, that I understood more of that language than I had imagined, which encouraged me to apply myself again to the study of it, and I met with more success, as those preceding languages had greatly smoothed my way.

"From these circumstances, I have thought that there is some inconsistency in our common mode of teaching languages. We are told that it is proper to begin first with the Latin, and, having acquired that, it will be more easy to attain those modern languages which are derived from it; and yet we do not begin with the Greek, in order more easily to acquire the Latin. It is true that, if we can clamber and get to the top of a staircase without using the steps, we shall more easily gain them in descending; but certainly if we begin with the lowest, we shall with more ease ascend to the top;

and I would therefore offer it to the consideration of those, who superintend the education of our youth, whether, since many of those who begin with the Latin, quit the same after spending some years without having made any great proficiency, and what they have learned becomes almost useless, so that their time has been lost, it would not have been better to have begun with the French, proceeding to the Italian and Latin. For though after spending the same time they should quit the study of languages and never arrive at the Latin, they would, however, have acquired another tongue or two, that, being in modern use, might be serviceable to them in common life." [2]

As of extreme importance in method, Franklin was always wont to stress the idea of self-activity, not just as a theory, but as a matter of practice. Indeed, we must learn of Franklin's ideas on the subject of education through his practice far more often than from theorizing.

Having failed in arithmetic, under the instruction of George Brownell, and being "ashamed of my ignorance in figures . . ." reliance was put on the self-active

[2] *The Life of Benjamin Franklin, Written by Himself,* pp. 109–110, New York, 1856.

METHODS AND AGENCIES OF SELF-EDUCATION

method of study. Taking Cocker's *Arithmetic,* he went through it by himself. Then he read Seller and Shermy on navigation and learned something of the science of geometry, ". . . but never proceeded far in that science."[3]

So it was, too, with his English style. He had early given evidence of a love of poetry but was discouraged in his efforts at verse-making by his father, who ridiculed him, saying that "verse-makers were generally beggars." Thus, he believed, he "escaped being a poet, most probably a very bad one." But that which was denied expression in rhyme was to be set free in winged, rhythmic prose, more forceful than any yet produced in the United States. To cultivate "what little ability" he modestly admitted was acquired in the latter, he relied upon the same active principle of self-education. Here is how it came about, he said:

"About this time I met with an odd volume of the *Spectator*. It was the third. I had never before seen any of them. I bought it, read it over and over, and was much delighted with it. I thought the writing excellent, and wished, if possible, to imitate it. With this view I

[3] For his thoughts on the value of mathematics, see pp. 229–235.

took some of the papers, and, making short hints of the sentiment in each sentence, laid them by a few days, and then, without looking at the book, tried to complete the papers again, by expressing each hinted sentiment at length, and as fully as it had been expressed before, in any suitable words that should come to hand. Then I compared my *Spectator* with the original, discovered some of my faults, and corrected them. But I found I wanted a stock of words, or a readiness in recollecting and using them, which I thought I should have acquired before that time if I had gone on making verses; since the continual occasion for words of the same import, but of different length, to suit the measure, or of different sound for the rhyme, would have laid me under a constant necessity of searching for variety, and also have tended to fix that variety in my mind, and make me master of it. Therefore I took some of the tales and turned them into verse; and, after a time, when I had pretty well forgotten the prose, turned them back again. I also sometimes jumbled my collections of hints into confusion, and after some weeks endeavored to reduce them into the best order, before I began to form the full sentences and complete the paper. This was to teach me method in the arrangement of thoughts. By comparing my work afterwards with the original, I discovered many faults and amended them; but I

METHODS AND AGENCIES OF SELF-EDUCATION

sometimes had the pleasure of fancying that, in certain particulars of small import, I had been lucky enough to improve the method or the language, and this encouraged me to think I might possibly in time come to be a tolerable English writer, of which I was extremely ambitious. My time for these exercises and for reading was at night, after work or before it began in the morning, or on Sundays, when I contrived to be in the printing-house alone, evading as much as I could the common attendance on public worship which my father used to exact of me when I was under his care, and which indeed I still thought a duty, though I could not, as it seemed to me, afford time to practice it." [4]

It was not alone in the study of school subjects, however, that this method was utilized. Indeed, throughout life Franklin continued his self-education, constantly carrying on observations, trying experiments, recording results; many of the projects he launched were simply the means of opening up further opportunities for self-education. In this connection, the Junto was founded.

The Leather-Apron Club, or Junto, "a club for mutual improvement," organized in 1727, was a monument

---

[4] BIGELOW, JOHN, *The Works of Benjamin Franklin,* Vol. I, pp. 50–52. (By permission of G. P. Putnam's Sons, publishers, New York, 1904.)

to Franklin's self-active method. He was its founder, guide, and inspiration. The purpose and method as stated in the *Autobiography,* follow:

"The rules that I drew up required that every member, in his turn, should produce one or more queries on any point of morals, politics, or natural philosophy, to be discussed by the company; and once in three months produce and read an essay of his own writing, on any subject he pleased. Our debates were to be under the direction of a president, and to be conducted in the sincere spirit of inquiry after truth, without fondness for dispute, or desire of victory; and, to prevent warmth, all expressions of positiveness in opinions, or direct contradiction, were after some time made contraband, and prohibited under small pecuniary penalties." [5]

That its instructional purpose was uppermost in Franklin's mind is seen in his opposition to increasing the members to more than twelve. At his suggestion that each member should become the leader of a new club, several others, such as The Vine, The Band, and The Union, came into existence. The Junto continued for about forty years and was financially a profitable

[5] *Ibid.,* p. 153.

METHODS AND AGENCIES OF SELF-EDUCATION

venture for Franklin, as well as an educative one, since numerous items of business came to him through these friends. Educationally, he regarded it as

". . . the best school of philosophy, morality, and politics that then existed in the province; for our queries, which were read the week preceding their discussion, put us upon reading with attention upon the several subjects, that we might speak more to the purpose; and here, too, we acquired better habits of conversation, everything being studied in our rules which might prevent our disgusting each other." [6]

When the American Philosophical Society, originated by Franklin, came into being (1744), a book containing many of the questions discussed by the Junto was given to William Smith, provost of the College, who published them in his *Eulogium on Franklin*. The following specimens indicate the social and scientific character of the discussions in this society for mutual improvement:

"Is sound an entity or body?
"How may the phenomena of vapors be explained?

[6] *Ibid.*, p. 154.

FRANKLIN'S EDUCATIONAL VIEWS

"Is self-interest the rudder that steers mankind, the universal monarch to whom all are tributaries?

"Which is the best form of government, and what was that form which first prevailed among mankind?

"Can any one particular form of government suit all mankind?

"What is the reason that the tides rise higher in the Bay of Fundy, than the Bay of Delaware?

"Is the emission of paper money safe?

"What is the reason that men of the greatest knowledge are not the most happy?

"How may the possessions of the Lakes be improved to our advantage?

"Why are tumultuous, uneasy sensations, united with our desires?

"Whether it ought to be the aim of philosophy to eradicate the passions?

"How may smoky chimneys be best cured?

"Why does the flame of a candle tend upwards in a spire?

"Which is least criminal, a bad action joined with a good intention, or a good action with a bad intention?

"Is it inconsistent with the principles of liberty in a free government, to punish a man as a libeller, when he speaks the truth?" [7]

[7] SPARKS, JARED, *The Works of Benjamin Franklin,* Vol. II, pp. 9-10, Boston, 1836-1840.

METHODS AND AGENCIES OF SELF-EDUCATION

These seem to emanate from a school of practical politics and of applied science. It is hard to imagine a more useful kind of association for one who was to play so well the leading rôles of statesman and scientist. The question of emitting paper money was alive. The public interest and the debates in the society possessed Franklin so completely that he published an anonymous pamphlet, *A Modest Enquiry into the Nature and Necessity of a Paper Currency* (1729), which, he says, "was well received by the common people in general." Likewise, certain of the scientific questions remained with him all his life. Thus we find him, on returning from France as successful plenipotentiary of the United States and world-renowned figure, sitting down to write a paper on "The Cause and Cure of Smoky Chimneys."

In 1728, the following set of "Rules for a Club Established for Mutual Improvement" were drawn up:

"Previous question, to be answered at every meeting.
"Have you read over these queries this morning, in order to consider what you might have to offer the Junto touching any one of them? Viz.
"1. Have you met with anything in the author you

last read, remarkable, or suitable to be communicated to the Junto? particularly in history, morality, poetry, physic, travels, mechanic arts, or other parts of knowledge.

"2. What new story have you lately heard agreeable for telling in conversation?

"3. Hath any citizen in your knowledge failed in his business lately, and what have you heard of the cause?

"4. Have you lately heard of any citizen's thriving well, and by what means?

"5. Have you lately heard how any present rich man, here or elsewhere, got his estate?

"6. Do you know of a fellow citizen, who has lately done a worthy action, deserving praise and imitation; or who has lately committed an error, proper for us to be warned against and avoid?

"7. What unhappy effects of intemperance have you lately observed or heard; of imprudence, of passion, or of any other vice or folly?

"8. What happy effects of temperance, of prudence, of moderation, or of any other virtue?

"9. Have you or any of your acquaintance been lately sick or wounded? If so, what remedies were used, and what were their effects?

"10. Whom do you know that are shortly going voy-

METHODS AND AGENCIES OF SELF-EDUCATION

ages or journeys, if one should have occasion to send by them?

"11. Do you think of anything at present, in which the Junto may be serviceable to mankind, to their country, to their friends, or to themselves?

"12. Hath any deserving stranger arrived in town since last meeting, that you have heard of? And what have you heard or observed of his character or merits? And whether, think you, it lies in the power of the Junto to oblige him, or encourage him as he deserves?

"13. Do you know of any deserving young beginner lately set up, whom it lies in the power of the Junto any way to encourage?

"14. Have you lately observed any defect in the laws of your country, of which it would be proper to move the legislature for an amendment? Or do you know of any beneficial law that is wanting?

"15. Have you lately observed any encroachment on the just liberties of the people?

"16. Hath anybody attacked your reputation lately? And what can the Junto do towards securing it?

"17. Is there any man whose friendship you want, and which the Junto, or any of them, can procure for you?

"18. Have you lately heard any member's character attacked, and how have you defended it?

"19. Hath any man injured you, from whom it is in the power of the Junto to procure redress?

"20. In what manner can the Junto, or any of them, assist you in any of your honorable designs?

"21. Have you any weighty affair on hand, in which you think the advice of the Junto may be of service?

"22. What benefits have you lately received from any man not present?

"23. Is there any difficulty in matters of opinion, of justice, and injustice, which you would gladly have discussed at this time?

"24. Do you see anything amiss in the present customs or proceedings of the Junto, which might be amended?" [8]

An interesting insight into the liberal tolerance and spirit of philosophic inquiry, so characteristic of Franklin, may be gained from the catechism to be answered, with hand on the breast, by those who were to be qualified as members of the Junto.

"1. Have you any particular disrespect to any present member? *Answer*. I have not.

"2. Do you sincerely declare, that you love mankind in general, of what profession or religion soever? *Answer*. I do.

[8] *Ibid.*, pp. 9–12.

"3. Do you think any person ought to be harmed in his body, name, or goods, for mere speculative opinions, or his external way of worship? *Answer.* No.

"4. Do you love truth for truth's sake, and will you endeavor impartially to find and receive it yourself, and communicate it to others? *Answer.* Yes." [9]

Franklin's most far-reaching services to American society were those which he institutionalized. His work did not pause with personal improvement or that of his immediate friends. Academies, colleges, libraries, hospitals, and scientific societies attest the wide range of his creative genius. But he accomplished so much only by working through his fellows. Here one meets again his faith in a proper method of doing things—a proper method of education in the broader, public sense. Franklin ever quoted with approval the lines of Pope:

Men should be taught as if you taught them not,
And things unknown proposed as things forgot.

It was by this method, moreover, that he continually instructed his fellow men. But it was from a study of the Socratic method, as exemplified in the *Memorabilia,* that he gained the conviction that this modest, diffident

[9] *Ibid.*

method was the most advantageous in inculcating opinions and persuading men to measures. He describes the discovery thus:

"While I was intent on improving my language, I met with an English grammar (I think it was Greenwood's), at the end of which there were two little sketches of the arts of rhetoric and logic, the latter finishing with a specimen of a dispute in the Socratic method, and soon after I procured Xenophon's *Memorable Things of Socrates,* wherein there are many instances of the same method. I was charmed with it, adopted it, dropped my abrupt contradiction and positive argumentation, and put on the humble inquirer and doubter. And being then, from reading Shaftesbury and Collins, become a real doubter in many points of our religious doctrine, I found this method safest for myself and very embarrassing to those against whom I used it; therefore I took a delight in it, practiced it continually, and grew very artful and expert in drawing people, even of superior knowledge, into concessions, the consequences of which they did not foresee, entangling them in difficulties out of which they could not extricate themselves, and so obtaining victories that neither myself nor my cause always deserved. I continued this method some few years, but gradually left

METHODS AND AGENCIES OF SELF-EDUCATION

it, retaining only the habit of expressing myself in terms of modest diffidence; never using, when I advanced anything that may possibly be disputed, the words certainly, undoubtedly, or any others that give the air of positiveness to an opinion, but rather say, I conceive or apprehend a thing to be so and so; it appears to me, or I should think it so or so, for such and such reasons; or I imagine it to be so; or it is so, if I am not mistaken. This habit, I believe, has been of great advantage to me when I have had occasion to inculcate my opinions, and persuade men into measures that I have been from time to time engaged in promoting; and, as the chief ends of conversation are to inform or to be informed, to please or to persuade, I wish well-meaning, sensible men would not lessen their power of doing good by a positive, assuming manner, that seldom fails to disgust, tends to create opposition, and to defeat every one of those purposes for which speech was given to us,—to wit, giving or receiving information or pleasure. For, if you would inform, a positive and dogmatical manner in advancing your sentiments may provoke contradiction and prevent a candid attention. If you wish information and improvement from the knowledge of others, and yet at the same time express yourself as firmly fixed in your present opinions, modest, sensible men, who do not love disputation, will probably leave you undisturbed in the possession of your error. And by such a manner, you can seldom hope to recommend yourself in pleasing your hearers, or to persuade those whose concurrence you desire."[10]

II

It would be interesting and instructive to make an inventory of the specific contributions of those relatively rare individuals, since the dawn of civilization, who have watched the water life in rippling pools, gazed in unwonted ecstasy at swaying chandeliers, been impressed by falling apples and steaming teapots, measured with professional care the temperature of the oceans, and scrutinized the habits of smoke in chimneys —just because these, which were so common to other men, were the most immediate, mysterious, and challenging facts of their environment at that particular moment. To these men the explanation of such common occurrences has seemed of vaster consequence than defining the nature of God, the sinfulness of nature, or

---

[10] BIGELOW, JOHN, *The Works of Benjamin Franklin,* Vol. I, pp. 53–55. (By permission of G. P. Putnam's Sons, publishers, New York, 1904.)

METHODS AND AGENCIES OF SELF-EDUCATION

the limits of the universe. Engaged in such a task, one would find the inventory of the eighteenth century crowded with the explorations of Benjamin Franklin whose mind, whenever free from routine labors of the day, leaped, as if drawn by a powerful magnet, to some earthy, practical, perplexing problem. Whirlwinds, waterspouts, balloons, stoves, the Gulf Stream, electrical fire, smoking chimneys, optics, medicine, finance, sundials, tides, absorption and reflection of heat, military science, silk culture, gardening, scientific agriculture, meteorology, and hydrostatics were among the things that interested him and to many of which he gave studious hours when not printing books, selling them, or serving in public offices. Utility was his first criterion; to do good, his purpose. One of the earliest pictures we have is of the boy Franklin leading his comrades in the construction of a small dike of building stones from which they might fish without wetting their feet. In another, one sees him harnessing the wind to tow him on his back across the water. After twenty, the more methodical man of science began to emerge; and Franklin, as was his wont, did not choose to travel the road alone. In 1727, the Junto was organized, in which scientific questions were discussed for the mutual improvement of its members. It also existed for the purpose of promoting practical, everyday business success of these friends. Franklin worked hard; but always with an eye to wealth and the leisure that could come to him only through it. As it happened, when he had gained wealth, he almost entirely sacrificed his leisure that he might serve the Colonies and his children the United States. But on those occasions when he was, perforce, idle, as on numerous ocean voyages, he turned to his first love, to observe, experiment, measure, and record.

Near the middle of the century, having settled himself well in the printing business, established the Library Company of Philadelphia, gained fame as author and publisher of *Poor Richard's Almanac,* and become postmaster of Philadelphia, he found enough freedom to set down definitely some conclusions about problems that had challenged his attention for years. In 1742, the Franklin open stove appeared; two years later, *An Account of the Newly Invented Pennsylvania Fire Places* was published; in 1745, his experiments with electrical fire were undertaken; and, in 1747, his theory of electrical phenomena was advanced. It was, significantly, while he was engaged in these researches that he gave first thought to the promotion of elementary scientific education for youth, as to which, in his judgment, Philadelphia had been negligent; and to a society (1743) which should promote scientific knowledge among "men of speculation" which might prove of advantage to "some or all of the British plantations, or to the benefit of mankind in general." The project undoubtedly appealed to him personally, for the hard labor of his earlier years was past; and, for the country at large, the time seemed propitious to him as "the first drudgery of settling new colonies . . ." was ". . . now pretty well over" and there were "many in every province in circumstances that set them at ease. . . ."

The American Philosophical Society, a larger and more scientific Junto, the first scientific society in the Colonies and forerunner of the American Association for the Advancement of Science, was established in 1744, according to the "Proposal" prepared by Franklin, dated May 14, 1743.

FRANKLIN'S EDUCATIONAL VIEWS

A PROPOSAL
FOR PROMOTING USEFUL KNOWLEDGE AMONG THE BRITISH
PLANTATIONS IN AMERICA

Philadelphia, 14 May, 1743.

The English are possessed of a long tract of continent, from Nova Scotia to Georgia, extending north and south through different climates, having different soils, producing different plants, mines, and minerals, and capable of different improvements, manufactures, etc.

The first drudgery of settling new colonies, which confines the attention of people to mere necessaries, is now pretty well over; and there are many in every province in circumstances that set them at ease, and afford leisure to cultivate the finer arts and improve the common stock of knowledge. To such of these who are men of speculation many hints must from time to time arise, many observations occur, which, if well examined, pursued, and improved, might produce discoveries to the advantage of some or all of the British plantations or to the benefit of mankind in general.

But as from the extent of the country such persons are widely separated, and seldom can see and converse or be acquainted with each other, so that many useful

METHODS AND AGENCIES OF SELF-EDUCATION

particulars remain uncommunicated, die with the discoverers, and are lost to mankind; it is, to remedy this inconvenience for the future, proposed:

That one society be formed of *virtuosi* or ingenious men residing in the several colonies, to be called *The American Philosophical Society,* who are to maintain a constant correspondence.

That Philadelphia, being the city nearest the centre of the continent colonies, communicating with all of them northward and southward by post, and with all the islands by sea, and having the advantage of a good growing library, be the centre of the Society.

That at Philadelphia there be always at least seven members, viz., a physician, a botanist, a mathematician, a chemist, a mechanician, a geographer, and a general natural philosopher, besides a president, treasurer, and secretary.

That these members meet once a month or oftener, at their own expense, to communicate to each other their observations and experiments; to receive, read, and consider such letters, communications, or queries as shall be sent from distant members; to direct the dispersing of copies of such communications as are valuable, to other distant members, in order to procure their sentiments thereupon.

That the subjects of the correspondence be: all new-

FRANKLIN'S EDUCATIONAL VIEWS

discovered plants, herbs, trees, roots, their virtues, uses, etc.; methods of propagating them, and making such as are useful, but particular to some plantations, more general; improvements of vegetable juices, as ciders, wines, etc.; new methods of curing or preventing diseases; all new-discovered fossils in different countries, as mines, minerals, and quarries; new and useful improvements in any branch of mathematics; new discoveries in chemistry, such as improvements in distillation, brewing, and assaying of ores; new mechanical inventions for saving labor, as mills and carriages, and for raising and conveying of water, draining of meadows, etc.; all new arts, trades, and manufactures that may be proposed or thought of; surveys, maps, and charts of particular parts of the sea-coasts or inland countries; course and junction of rivers and great roads, situation of lakes and mountains, nature of the soil and productions; new methods of improving the breed of useful animals; introducing other sorts from foreign countries; new improvements in planting, gardening, and clearing land; and all philosophical experiments that let light into the nature of things, tend to increase the power of man over matter and multiply the conveniences or pleasures of life.

That a correspondence already begun by some intended members shall be kept up by this Society with the ROYAL SOCIETY of London and with the DUBLIN SOCIETY.

That every member shall have abstracts sent him quarterly of everything valuable communicated to the Society's Secretary at Philadelphia, free of all charge, except the yearly payment hereafter mentioned.

That, by permission of the postmaster-general, such communications pass between the Secretary of the Society and the members, postage-free.

That, for defraying the expense of such experiments as the Society shall judge proper to cause to be made, and other contingent charges for the common good, every member send a piece of eight per annum to the treasurer, at Philadelphia, to form a common stock, to be disbursed by order of the President, with the consent of the majority of the members that can conveniently be consulted thereupon, to such persons and places where and by whom the experiments are to be made, and otherwise as there shall be occasion; of which disbursements an exact account shall be kept, and communicated yearly to every member.

That, at the first meetings of the members at Philadelphia, such rules be formed for regulating their meetings and transactions for the general benefit as shall be convenient and necessary; to be afterwards changed and improved as there shall be occasion, wherein due regard is to be had to the advice of distant members.

That, at the end of every year, collections be made and printed of such experiments, discoveries, and improvements as may be thought of public advantage; and that every member have a copy sent him.

That the business and duty of the Secretary be to receive all letters intended for the Society, and lay them before the President and members at their meetings; to abstract, correct, and methodize such papers as require it, and as he shall be directed to do by the President, after they have been considered, debated, and digested in the Society; to enter copies thereof in the Society's books, and make out copies for distant members; to answer their letters by direction of the President; and keep records of all material transactions of the Society.

Benjamin Franklin, the writer of this Proposal, offers himself to serve the Society as their secretary, till they shall be provided with one more capable.[11]

---

[11] "This paper appears to contain the first suggestion, in any public form, for an *American Philosophical Society.*" JOHN BIGELOW, *The Works of Benjamin Franklin,* Vol. II, pp. 67–71. (By permission of G. P. Putnam's Sons, publishers, New York, 1904.)

METHODS AND AGENCIES OF SELF-EDUCATION

III

If we consider, according to a modern interpretation, that all is educational which results in a control or influence over conduct, and were to include all those papers by Franklin which were thus influential, this small volume would have to be expanded to several. Many essays of a strictly and narrowly scientific character would have to be included, for they taught and inspired his fellow journeymen of science and invention. But we shall pass them by, leaving those interested in the specific, scientific lessons he taught to consult complete editions of his letters and pamphlets. His papers that were most specifically educational may be put into three classes: first, those dealing with means of formal school education; second, those dealing with adult, self-education and research in the scientific sense, illustrated by the "Proposal" which led to founding the American Philosophical Society; and, third, those publications dealing with adult education of the everyday, home-grown, prudential variety. The latter really were sermons on industry and economy. They were not delivered to pedagogues assembled in solemn, sleepy, conclaves; instead, they, like the influential example of a fellow apprentice, journeyman, or master, carried a concise, vigorous, compelling message to every aspiring body who sought like Franklin to plant his feet on the solid ground of financial independence. To John Alleyne, he wrote: "Be studious in your profession, and you will be learned. Be industrious and frugal, and you will be rich. Be sober and temperate, and you will be healthy. Be in general virtuous, and you will be happy."[12] In these few lines, was summed up most that he had to say in such papers as "Advice to a Young Tradesman" (1748) and the "Speech of Father Abraham" or "The Way to Wealth" (1757). Of all the papers giving expression to this prudential wisdom and instruction, the two just mentioned are given here.

Advice to a Young Tradesman
Written in the Year 1748

To My Friend, A. B.,

As you have desired it of me, I write the following

[12] From Smyth, A. H., *The Writings of Benjamin Franklin,* Vol. V, p. 159. (By permission of The Macmillan Company, publishers, New York, 1905.)

METHODS AND AGENCIES OF SELF-EDUCATION

hints, which have been of service to me, and may, if observed, be so to you.

Remember, that time is money. He that can earn ten shillings a day by his labor, and goes abroad, or sits idle, one half of that day, though he spends but sixpence during his diversion or idleness, ought not to reckon that the only expense; he has really spent, or rather thrown away, five shillings besides.

Remember, that credit is money. If a man lets his money lie in my hands after it is due, he gives me the interest, or so much as I can make of it during that time. This amounts to a considerable sum where a man has good and large credit, and makes good use of it.

Remember, that money is of the prolific, generating nature. Money can beget money, and its offspring can beget more, and so on. Five shillings turned is six, turned again it is seven and threepence, and so on till it becomes an hundred pounds. The more there is of it, the more it produces every turning, so that the profits rise quicker and quicker. He that kills a breeding sow, destroys all her offspring to the thousandth generation. He that murders a crown, destroys all that it might have produced, even scores of pounds.

Remember, that six pounds a year is but a groat a day. For this little sum (which may be daily wasted either in time or expense unperceived) a man of credit may on

FRANKLIN'S EDUCATIONAL VIEWS

his own security, have the constant possession and use of an hundred pounds. So much in stock, briskly turned by an industrious man, produces great advantage.

Remember this saying, "The good paymaster is lord of another man's purse." He that is known to pay punctually and exactly to the time he promises, may at any time, and on any occasion, raise all the money his friends can spare. This is sometimes of great use. After industry and frugality, nothing contributes more to the raising of a young man in the world than punctuality and justice in all his dealings; therefore never keep borrowed money an hour beyond the time you promised, lest a disappointment shut up your friend's purse forever.

The most trifling actions that affect a man's credit are to be regarded. The sound of your hammer at five in the morning, or nine at night, heard by a creditor, makes him easy six months longer; but, if he sees you at a billiard-table, or hears your voice at a tavern, when you should be at work, he sends for his money the next day; demands it, before he can receive it, in a lump.

It shows, besides, that you are mindful of what you owe; it makes you appear a careful as well as an honest man, and that still increases your credit.

Beware of thinking all your own that you possess, and of living accordingly. It is a mistake that many people who have credit fall into. To prevent this, keep

METHODS AND AGENCIES OF SELF-EDUCATION

an exact account for some time, both of your expenses and your income. If you take the pains at first to mention particulars, it will have this good effect; you will discover how wonderfully small, trifling expenses mount up to large sums, and will discern what might have been, and may for the future be saved, without occasioning any great inconvenience.

In short, the way to wealth, if you desire it, is as plain as the way to market. It depends chiefly on two words, industry and frugality; that is, waste neither time nor money, but make the best use of both. Without industry and frugality nothing will do, and with them everything. He that gets all he can honestly, and saves all he gets (necessary expenses excepted), will certainly become rich, if that Being who governs the world, to whom all should look for a blessing on their honest endeavors, doth not, in his wise providence, otherwise determine. AN OLD TRADESMAN.[13]

THE WAY TO WEALTH [14]

COURTEOUS READER,

I have heard that nothing gives an author so great

[13] SPARKS, JARED, *The Works of Benjamin Franklin,* Vol. II, pp. 87-89, Boston, 1836-1840.

[14] From *The Sayings of Poor Richard,* pp. 268-283, ed. by Paul Leicester Ford, Brooklyn, 1890. (Used by permission of Mrs. Linsly R. Williams.)

FRANKLIN'S EDUCATIONAL VIEWS

pleasure, as to find his works respectfully quoted by other learned authors. This pleasure I have seldom enjoyed, for though I have been, if I may say it without vanity, an eminent author of almanacs annually now a full quarter of a century, my brother authors in the same way, for what reason I know not, have ever been very sparing in their applauses; and no other author has taken the least notice of me, so that did not my writings produce me some solid pudding, the great deficiency of praise would have quite discouraged me.

I concluded at length, that the people were the best judges of my merit; for they buy my works; and besides, in my rambles, where I am not personally known, I have frequently heard one or other of my adages repeated, with, "as Poor Richard says," at the end on 't; this gave me some satisfaction, as it showed not only that my instructions were regarded, but discovered likewise some respect for my authority; and I own that to encourage the practice of remembering and repeating those wise sentences, I have sometimes quoted myself with great gravity.

Judge then how much I must have been gratified by an incident I am going to relate to you. I stopped my horse lately where a great number of people were collected at a vendue of merchant goods. The hour of sale not being come, they were conversing on the badness

METHODS AND AGENCIES OF SELF-EDUCATION

of the times, and one of the company called to a plain clean old man, with white locks, "Pray Father Abraham, what think you of the times? Won't these heavy taxes quite ruin the country? How shall we be ever able to pay them? What would you advise us to?" Father Abraham stood up, and replied, "If you'd have my advice, I'll give it you in short, for 'a word to the wise is enough, and many words won't fill a bushel,' as Poor Richard says. . . ." They joined in desiring him to speak his mind, and gathering round him, he proceeded as follows:

"Friends," says he, "and neighbors, the taxes are indeed very heavy, and if those laid on by the government were the only ones we had to pay, we might more easily discharge them; but we have many others, and much more grievous to some of us. We are taxed twice as much by our idleness, three times as much by our pride, and four times as much by our folly, and from these taxes the commissioners cannot ease or deliver us by allowing an abatement. However, let us hearken to good advice, and something may be done for us; 'God helps them that help themselves,' as Poor Richard says in his Almanac of 1733.

"It would be thought a hard government that should tax its people one tenth part of their time, to be employed in its service. But idleness taxes many of us much more, if we reckon all that is spent in absolute sloth, or doing of nothing, with that which is spent in idle employments or amusements, that amount to nothing. Sloth, by bringing on diseases, absolutely shortens life. 'Sloth, like rust, consumes faster than labor wears, while the used key is always bright,' as Poor Richard says. But 'dost thou love life, then do not squander time, for that's the stuff life is made of,' as Poor Richard says.—How much more than is necessary do we spend in sleep! Forgetting that 'The sleeping fox catches no poultry,' and that 'there will be sleeping enough in the grave,' as Poor Richard says. If time be of all things the most precious, 'wasting of time must be,' as Poor Richard says, 'the greatest prodigality,' since, as he elsewhere tells us, 'Lost time is never found again'; and what we call 'time enough, always proves little enough.' Let us then be up and doing, and doing to the purpose; so by diligence shall we do more with less perplexity. 'Sloth makes all things difficult, but industry all things easy,' as Poor Richard says; and 'he that rises late, must trot all day, and shall scarce overtake his business at night.' While 'Laziness travels so slowly, that poverty soon overtakes him,' as we read in Poor Richard, who adds, 'Drive thy business, let not that drive thee; and early to bed, and early to rise, makes a man healthy, wealthy, and wise.'

METHODS AND AGENCIES OF SELF-EDUCATION

"So what signifies wishing and hoping for better times. We may make these times better if we bestir ourselves. 'Industry need not wish' as Poor Richard says, and 'He that lives upon hope will die fasting. There are no gains without pains'; then 'Help hands, for I have no lands,' or if I have, they are smartly taxed. And as Poor Richard likewise observes, 'He that hath a trade hath an estate,' and 'He that hath a calling hath an office of profit and honor'; but then the trade must be worked at, and the calling well followed, or neither the estate, nor the office, will enable us to pay our taxes.— If we are industrious we shall never starve; for as Poor Richard says, 'At the working man's house hunger looks in, but dares not enter.' Nor will the bailiff or the constable enter, for 'Industry pays debts while despair increases them,' says Poor Richard.—What though you have found no treasure, nor has any rich relation left you a legacy, 'Diligence is the mother of good luck,' as Poor Richard says, 'and God gives all things to industry.' Then 'plough deep, while sluggards sleep, and you shall have corn to sell and to keep,' says Poor Dick. Work while it is called today, for you know not how much you may be hindered tomorrow, which makes Poor Richard say, 'One today is worth two tomorrows'; and farther, 'Have you somewhat to do tomorrow, do it today.' If you were a servant would you not be ashamed that a good master should catch you idle? Are you then your own master, 'be ashamed to catch yourself idle,' as Poor Dick says. When there is so much to be done for yourself, your family, your country, and your gracious king, be up by peep of day; 'Let not the sun look down and say, inglorious here he lies.' Handle your tools without mittens; remember that 'the cat in gloves catches no mice,' as Poor Richard says. 'Tis true there is much to be done, and perhaps you are weak-handed, but stick to it steadily, and you will see great effects, for 'constant dropping wears away stones,' and by 'diligence and patience, the mouse ate in two the cable'; and 'Little strokes fell great oaks,' as Poor Richard says in his Almanac, the year I cannot just now remember.

"Methinks I hear some of you say, 'Must a man afford himself no leisure?'—I will tell thee, my friend, what Poor Richard says, 'Employ thy time well if thou meanest to gain leisure'; and, 'since thou art not sure of a minute, throw not away an hour.' Leisure is time for doing something useful; this leisure the diligent man will obtain, but the lazy man never; so that, as Poor Richard says, 'A life of leisure and a life of laziness are two things.' Do you imagine that sloth will afford you more comfort than labor? No, for as Poor

METHODS AND AGENCIES OF SELF-EDUCATION

Richard says, 'Trouble springs from idleness, and grievous toil from needless ease. Many without labor, would live by their wits only, but they break for want of stock.' Whereas industry gives comfort, and plenty and respect: 'Fly pleasures and they'll follow you. The diligent spinner has a large shift; and now I have a sheep and a cow, everybody bids me good morrow,' all which is well said by Poor Richard.

"But with our industry, we must likewise be steady, settled, and careful, and oversee our own affairs with our own eyes, and not trust too much to others; for, as Poor Richard says,

> *'I never saw an oft removed tree,*
> *Nor yet an oft removed family,*
> *That throve so well as those that settled be.'*

And again, 'Three removes is as bad as a fire'; and again, 'Keep thy shop, and thy shop will keep thee'; and again, 'If you would have your business done, go; if not, send.' And again,

> *'He that by the plough must thrive,*
> *Himself must either hold or drive.'*

And again, 'The eye of a master will do more work than both his hands'; and again, 'Want of care does us more damage than want of knowledge'; and again, 'Not to oversee workmen, is to leave them your purse open.' Trusting too much to others' care is the ruin of many; for, as the Almanac says, 'In the affairs of this world, men are saved, not by faith, but by the want of it'; but a man's own care is profitable; for, saith Poor Dick, 'Learning is to the studious,' and 'Riches to the careful,' as well as 'Power to the bold,' and 'Heaven to the virtuous.' And, farther, 'If you would have a faithful servant, and one that you like, serve yourself.' And again, he advises to circumspection and care, even in the smallest matters, because sometimes 'a little neglect may breed great mischief,' adding, 'for want of a nail, the shoe was lost; for want of a shoe the horse was lost; and for want of a horse the rider was lost,' being overtaken and slain by the enemy, all for want of care about a horseshoe nail.

"So much for industry, my friends, and attention to one's own business; but to these we must add frugality, if we would make our industry more certainly successful. A man may, if he knows not how to save as he gets, 'keep his nose all his life to the grindstone,' and die not worth a groat at last. 'A fat kitchen makes a lean will,' as Poor Richard says, and

A SKETCH OF FRANKLIN'S LIFE

ability, unbounded confidence in himself, and hopes in the future. After an illness which overtook both Denham and himself, a new life began. He set himself upon a determined course of self-education, rigid discipline, and economy.

Franklin's success in building institutions was founded on his success in building his own personal fortune. This, though not colossal, was large for the eighteenth century. Contemplating his rapid rise to independent wealth, one is apt to believe it was all an easy matter. But such was not the case. No sooner did he feel his feet on solid rock, when he had begun work for Mr. Denham, than all was changed in a trice. Mr. Denham died and Franklin escaped narrowly. The former failing to leave him anything, he had to go back to Keimer, the printer. In this connection, he made a friend, Meredith, one of the first members of the Junto, with whose father's assistance they were able to set up a shop of their own. This they opened in 1728, and George House, a friend in the Junto, brought in their first customer, who inserted a five-shilling advertisement. Brientnall, another member, did likewise, bringing considerable custom from his Quaker friends. It

FRANKLIN'S EDUCATIONAL VIEWS

became evident shortly, however, that Meredith's father could not advance enough money to pay for the equipment, and their creditor made suit against them. Fortunately for Franklin, two friends, Grace and Coleman, also of the Junto, offered to loan enough to enable him to take over the entire shop, leaving his partner Meredith free. Thus, consolidating his debts, he became, at twenty-four, owner of his own shop. He obtained the job of printing the Newcastle paper money, opened a stationery shop, and—to impress his creditors— ". . . never went out afishing or shooting . . . ," dressed plainly and sometimes carried to his shop in a wheelbarrow the paper he had bought in the stores. Now, he said, things ". . . went on swimmingly."

It was at this time that Benjamin's thought turned to the necessity of marriage. It might be, he thought, an asset. Rejected by the Godfreys because he asked a hundred pounds with their daughter, he made overtures elsewhere but found that, "the business of printer being generally thought a poor one . . ." it was useless to expect a dowry. Till then, it does not appear that he had thought of Deborah Read, who had married when he went to England and had been deserted by her

A SKETCH OF FRANKLIN'S LIFE

worthless husband. Whether he "pitied poor Miss Read's unfortunate situation . . ." more or liked his own lonely life less is not quite clear from his record. But he ". . . took her to wife, September 1st, 1730." She was a good, thrifty mate, took in his son William Franklin, helped in the shop while Franklin got out the printing business, and looked after his affairs thoroughly while he was away. To them were born Francis Folger and a daughter, Sarah. Deborah died, 1774, just before his return from England. To "Debby," his "Dear Child," Franklin wrote many letters which show the regard he had for her. He wrote, in the *Autobiography*, ". . . we throve together and have ever mutually endeavored to make each other happy."

Franklin's business expanded. In 1732, he began publication of *Poor Richard's Almanac,* which averaged 10,000 copies a year till 1758. The *Philadelphia Zeitung,* also, had its beginning the same year. In 1733, a branch printing establishment was opened in Charleston, South Carolina. In 1741, in company with James Parker, he opened a printing shop in New York. In Jamaica, Antigua, and the Dominican Islands his interests flourished under the hands of his trusted men. Dunlap, at Lancaster, James Franklin, in Newport, and Armbruster, in the German firm at Philadelphia, promoted his printing interests. By 1748, just eighteen years after he became sole owner of his printing shop, he was able to dispose of the business to David Hall, his partner, and retire from active work with a comfortable fortune. When Franklin died, his estate was worth approximately $150,000.

In a letter to his mother, Franklin wrote, in the days of increasing ease, ". . . the last will come when I would rather have it said, he lived usefully, than he died rich." Both could be said with equal truth. As soon as leisure was at his command, it was used for the promotion of science and the public good. In the decade of the forties, this became increasingly evident.

IV

Self-education he sought to promote by bringing others to his system and founding the Junto, a society for mutual improvement. But its purpose was mutual aid as well as improvement. Franklin was often to thank his friends of the Junto for favors in business as well

METHODS AND AGENCIES OF SELF-EDUCATION

'Many estates are spent in the getting,
Since women for tea forsook spinning and knitting,
And men for punch forsook hewing and splitting.'

'If you would be wealthy,' says he, in another Almanac, 'think of saving, as well as of getting: The Indies have not made Spain rich, because her outgoes are greater than her incomes.' Away then with your expensive follies, you will not have so much cause to complain of hard times, heavy taxes, and chargeable families; for as Poor Dick says,

'Women and wine, game and deceit,
Make the wealth small and the wants great.'

And farther, 'What maintains one vice would bring up two children.' You may think perhaps that a little tea or a little punch now and then, diet a little more costly, clothes a little finer, and a little entertainment now and then, can be no great matter; but remember what Poor Richard says, 'Many a little makes a mickle'; and farther, 'Beware of little expenses; a small leak will sink a great ship'; and again, 'Who dainties love shall beggars prove'; and moreover, 'Fools make feasts and wise men eat them.'

FRANKLIN'S EDUCATIONAL VIEWS

"Here you are all got together at this vendue of fineries and knicknacks. You call them goods, but if you do not take care, they will prove evils to some of you. You expect they will be sold cheap, and perhaps they may for less than they cost; but if you have no occasion for them, they must be dear to you. Remember what Poor Richard says, 'Buy what thou hast no need of, and ere long thou shalt sell thy necessaries.' And again, 'At a great pennyworth pause a while': He means, that perhaps the cheapness is apparent only, and not real; or the bargain, by straitening thee in thy business, may do thee more harm than good. For in another place he says, 'Many have been ruined by buying good pennyworths.' Again Poor Richard says, ' 'Tis foolish to lay out money in a purchase of repentance'; and yet this folly is practiced every day at vendues, for want of minding the Almanac. 'Wise men,' as Poor Dick says, 'learn by others' harms, fools scarcely by their own'; but *'Felix quem faciunt aliena pericula cautum.'* Many a one, for the sake of finery on the back, have gone with a hungry belly, and half-starved their families; 'Silks and satins, scarlet and velvets,' as Poor Richard says, 'put out the kitchen fire.' These are not the necessaries of life; they can scarcely be called the conveniences, and yet only because they look pretty how many want to have them. The artificial wants of mankind thus become more numerous than the natural; and as Poor Dick says, 'For one poor person there are an hundred indigent.' By these, and other extravagances, the genteel are reduced to poverty, and forced to borrow of those whom they formerly despised, but who through industry and frugality have maintained their standing; in which case it appears plainly, that a 'ploughman on his legs is higher than a gentleman on his knees,' as Poor Richard says. Perhaps they have had a small estate left them, which they knew not the getting of,—they think ' 'tis day and will never be night; that a little to be spent out of so much, is not worth minding; ('a child and a fool,' as Poor Richard says, 'imagine twenty shillings and twenty years can never be spent') but, always taking out of the meat-tub, and never putting in, soon comes to the bottom'; then, as Poor Dick says, 'When the well's dry, they know the worth of water.' But this they might have known before, if they had taken his advice; 'If you would know the value of money, go and try to borrow some; for he that goes a borrowing goes a sorrowing'; and indeed so does he that lends to such people, when he goes to get it in again.—Poor Dick farther advises, and says,

'Fond pride of dress, is sure a very curse;
E'er fancy you consult, consult your purse.'

And again, 'Pride is as loud a beggar as want, and a great deal more saucy.' When you have bought one fine thing you must buy ten more, that your appearance may be all of a piece; but Poor Dick says, ' 'Tis easier to suppress the first desire, than to satisfy all that follow it.' And 'tis as truly folly for the poor to ape the rich, as for the frog to swell, in order to equal the ox.

> *'Great estates may venture more,*
> *But little boats should keep near shore.'*

'Tis however a folly soon punished; for 'Pride that dines on vanity sups on contempt,' as Poor Richard says. And in another place, 'Pride breakfasted with plenty, dined with poverty, and supped with infamy.' And after all, of what use is this pride of appearance, for which so much is risked, so much is suffered! It cannot promote health, or ease pain; it makes no increase of merit in the person, creates envy, it hastens misfortune.

> *'What is a butterfly? At best*
> *He's but a caterpillar drest.*
> *The gaudy fop's his picture just,'*

as Poor Richard says.

"But what madness must it be to run in debt for these

superfluities! We are offered by the terms of this vendue, six months credit; and that perhaps has induced some of us to attend it, because we cannot spare the ready money, and hope now to be fine without it. But, ah, think what you do when you run in debt: You give to another power over your liberty. If you cannot pay at the time, you will be ashamed to see your creditor; you will be in fear when you speak to him; you will make poor pitiful sneaking excuses, and by degrees come to lose your veracity, and sink into base downright lying; for as Poor Richard says, 'The second vice is lying, the first is running in debt.' And again, to the same purpose, 'Lying rides upon debt's back.' Whereas a freeborn Englishman ought not to be ashamed or afraid to see or speak to any man living. But poverty often deprives a man of all spirit and virtue; ' 'Tis hard for an empty bag to stand upright,' as Poor Richard truly says. What would you think of that prince, or that government, who should issue an edict forbidding you to dress like a gentleman, or a gentlewoman, on pain of imprisonment or servitude! Would you not say, that you are free, have a right to dress as you please, and that such an edict would be a breach of your privileges, and such a government tyrannical! And yet you are about to put yourself under that tyranny when you run in debt for such dress! Your creditor has authority at his pleasure to deprive you of your liberty, by confining you in gaol for life, or to sell you for a servant, if you should not be able to pay him! When you have got your bargain, you may, perhaps, think little of payment! But 'Creditors,' Poor Richard tells us, 'have better memories than debtors'; and in another place says, 'Creditors are a superstitious sect, great observers of set days and times. The day comes round before you are aware, and the demand is made before you are prepared to satisfy it, or if you bear your debt in mind, the term which at first seemed so long, will, as it lessens, appear extremely short.' Time will seem to have added wings to his heels as well as shoulders. 'Those have a short Lent,' saith Poor Richard, 'who owe money to be paid at Easter.' Then, since as he says, 'The borrower is a slave to the lender, and the debtor is the creditor,' disdain the chain, preserve your freedom; and maintain your independency; be industrious and free; be frugal and free. At present, perhaps, you may think yourself in thriving circumstances, and that you can bear a little extravagance without injury; but,

'For age and want save while you may;
No morning sun lasts a whole day,'

as Poor Richard says.—Gain may be temporary and uncertain, but ever while you live experience is constant and certain; and ' 'tis easier to build two chimneys than to keep one in fuel,' as Poor Richard says. 'So rather go to bed supperless than rise in debt.'

'Get what you can, and what you get hold.
'Tis the stone that will turn all your lead into gold,'

as Poor Richard says. And when you have got the Philosopher's Stone, sure you will no longer complain of the bad times, or the difficulty of paying taxes.

"This doctrine, my friends, is reason and wisdom; but after all, do not depend too much on your own industry, and frugality, and prudence, though excellent things; for they may all be blasted without the blessing of heaven; and therefore ask that blessing humbly, and be not uncharitable to those that at present seem to want it, but comfort and help them. Remember Job suffered and was afterwards prosperous.

"And now to conclude, 'Experience keeps a dear school, but fools will learn in no other, and scarce in that'; for it is true, 'we may give advice, but we cannot give conduct,' as Poor Richard says: However, remember this, 'They that won't be counselled, can't be helped,' as Poor Richard says: and farther, that 'if you will not hear Reason, she'll surely rap your knuckles.'"

Thus the old gentleman ended his harangue. The people heard it, and approved the doctrine, and immediately practiced the contrary, just as if it had been a common sermon; for the vendue opened, and they began to buy extravagantly, notwithstanding all his cautions, and their own fear of taxes.—I found the good man had thoroughly studied my almanacs, and digested all I had dropped on those topics during the course of five and twenty years. The frequent mention he made of me must have tired any one else, but my vanity was wonderfully delighted with it, though I was conscious that not a tenth part of this wisdom was my own which he ascribed to me, but rather the gleanings I had made of the sense of all ages and nations. However, I resolved to be the better for the echo of it; and though I had at first determined to buy stuff for a new coat, I went away resolved to wear my old one a little longer. Reader, if thou wilt do the same, thy profit will be as great as mine.

>I am as ever,
>   Thine to serve thee,
>   RICHARD SAUNDERS.

July 7, 1757.

METHODS AND AGENCIES OF SELF-EDUCATION

IV

On contemplating the foregoing "Proposals," "Rules," "Advice," and so forth, which Franklin so generously offered to others, the critical student has doubtless often wondered how successful the author would have been in taking his own advice. His prudential wisdom, health hints, and many other features were pretty firmly rooted in his everyday life, though he owed many of his ideas to Tryon; but the orderly plan for checking up his moral improvement indicates what he strove for, rather than attained. Franklin continues, in his *Autobiography*, to point out that his scheme of order gave him greatest trouble; that, indeed, for a man in his business, it was impossible to follow such a strict order of the day. "In truth," he added, "I found myself incorrigible with respect to order; and now I am grown old, and my memory bad, I feel very sensibly the want of it."

The list of virtues, at first, contained twelve. After careful examination, for some time, Franklin wrote, "I was surprised to find myself so much fuller of faults than I had imagined; but I had the satisfaction of seeing them diminish." Franklin informs us that to this system he owed the felicity he attained throughout life. To temperance he ascribed good health, long continued; to his industry and frugality, his fortune and all else that had enabled him to be a useful citizen and a man esteemed by others for his learning. He remarks particularly upon the fact that his scheme "was not wholly without religion" though it lacked the impress of any sectarian influence. The latter he purposely avoided, thinking the system might be of equal use to all people, regardless of religious persuasion. Franklin frequently referred to an intention to publish a book, *The Art of Virtue,* but this was never accomplished.

One of the virtues, humility, which proved to be the greatest stumbling block to his success, was added as number thirteen after a Quaker friend had informed him that he was generally thought proud. To correct the error, Franklin asserts, he forbade himself the use of expressions implying a fixed opinion. Nevertheless, he sagaciously remarked, he had little success in attaining the reality of humility, though a good deal in cultivating "the appearance of it." When writing at Passy, near the end of his life, he found that "disguise it, struggle with it, beat it down, stifle it, mortify it as much as one pleases, it is still alive, and will ever now and then jump out and show itself . . ." In fact, Franklin became so convinced as to the impossibility of a final victory over his black beast, that he believed if he could imagine he had overcome it, he would then become proud of his humility.

The substantial part of his system of moral education is given below, as he described it. No better example could be found to illustrate Franklin's efforts at self-education.

It was about this time I conceived the bold and arduous project of arriving at moral perfection. I wished to live without committing any fault at any time; I would conquer all that either natural inclination, custom, or company might lead me into. As I knew, or thought I knew, what was right and wrong, I did not see why I might not always do the one and avoid the other. But I soon found I had undertaken a task of more difficulty than I had imagined. While my care was employed in guarding against one fault, I was often surprised by another; habit took the advantage of inattention; inclination was sometimes too strong for reason. I concluded, at length, that the mere speculative conviction that it was our interest to be completely virtuous, was not sufficient to prevent our slipping; and that the contrary habits must be broken, and good ones acquired and established, before we can have any dependence on a steady, uniform rectitude of conduct. For this purpose I therefore contrived the following method.

In the various enumerations of the moral virtues I had met with in my reading, I found the catalogue more or less numerous, as different writers included more or fewer ideas under the same name. Temperance, for example, was by some confined to eating and drinking, while by others it was extended to mean the moderating every pleasure, appetite, inclination, or passion, bodily or mental, even to our avarice and ambition. I proposed to myself, for the sake of clearness, to use rather more names, with fewer ideas annexed to each, than a few names with more ideas; and I included under thirteen names of virtues all that at that time occurred to me as necessary or desirable, and annexed to each a short precept, which fully expressed the extent I gave to its meaning.

These names of virtues, with their precepts, were:

METHODS AND AGENCIES OF SELF-EDUCATION

1. Temperance

Eat not to dullness; drink not to elevation.

2. Silence

Speak not but what may benefit others or yourself; avoid trifling conversation.

3. Order

Let all your things have their places; let each part of your business have its time.

4. Resolution

Resolve to perform what you ought; perform without fail what you resolve.

5. Frugality

Make no expense but to do good to others or yourself; *i.e.,* waste nothing.

6. Industry

Lose no time; be always employed in something useful; cut off all unnecessary actions.

7. Sincerity

Use no hurtful deceit; think innocently and justly; and, if you speak, speak accordingly.

8. Justice

Wrong none by doing injuries, or omitting the benefits that are your duty.

9. Moderation

Avoid extremes; forbear resenting injuries so much as you think they deserve.

10. *Cleanliness*

Tolerate no uncleanliness in body, clothes, or habitation.

11. *Tranquillity*

Be not disturbed at trifles, or at accidents common or unavoidable.

12. *Chastity*

Rarely use venery but for health or offspring, never to dullness, weakness, or the injury of your own or another's peace or reputation.

13. *Humility*

Imitate Jesus and Socrates.

My intention being to acquire the habitude of all these virtues, I judged it would be well not to distract my attention by attempting the whole at once, but to fix it on one of them at a time; and, when I should be master of that, then proceed to another, and so on till I had gone through the thirteen; and, as the previous acquisition of some might facilitate the acquisition of certain others, I arranged them with that view, as they stand above. Temperance first, as it tends to procure that coolness and clearness of head, which is so necessary where constant vigilance was to be kept up, and guard maintained against the unremitting attraction of ancient habits, and the force of perpetual temptations. This being acquired and established, silence would be more easy; and my desire being to gain knowledge at the same time that I improved in virtue, and considering that in conversation it was obtained rather by the use of the ears than of the tongue, and therefore wishing to break a habit I was getting into of prattling, punning, and joking, which only made me acceptable to trifling company, I gave silence the second place. This and the next, order, I expected would allow me more time for attending to my project and my studies. Resolution, once become habitual, would keep me firm in my endeavors to obtain all the subsequent virtues; frugality and industry freeing me from my remaining debt, and producing affluence and independence, would make more easy the practice of sincerity and justice, etc., etc. Conceiving, then, that, agreeably to the advice of Pythagoras in his *Golden Verses,* daily examination would be necessary, I contrived the following method for conducting that examination.

I made a little book, in which I allotted a page for each of the virtues.[15] I ruled each page with red ink, so as to have seven columns, one for each day of the week, marking each column with a letter for the day. I crossed these columns with thirteen red lines, marking the beginning of each line with the first letter of one of the virtues, on which line, and in its proper column,

[15] This "little book" is dated July 1, 1733.

FRANKLIN'S EDUCATIONAL VIEWS

I might mark, by a little black spot, every fault I found upon examination to have been committed respecting that virtue upon that day.

Form of the Pages

TEMPERANCE.

EAT NOT TO DULLNESS;
DRINK NOT TO ELEVATION.

	S.	M.	T.	W.	T.	F.	S.
T.							
S.	*	*		*		*	
O.	**	*	*		*	*	*
R.			*			*	
F.		*			*		
I.			*				
S.							
J.							
M.							
C.							
T.							
C.							
H.							

I determined to give a week's strict attention to each of the virtues successively. Thus, in the first week, my

METHODS AND AGENCIES OF SELF-EDUCATION

great guard was to avoid every the least offence against temperance, leaving the other virtues to their ordinary chance, only marking every evening the faults of the day. Thus, if in the first week I could keep my first line, marked T, clear of spots, I supposed the habit of that virtue so much strengthened, and its opposite weakened, that I might venture extending my attention to include the next, and for the following week keep both lines clear of spots. Proceeding thus to the last, I could go through a course complete in thirteen weeks, and four courses in a year. And like him who, having a garden to weed, does not attempt to eradicate all the bad herbs at once, which would exceed his reach and his strength, but works on one of the beds at a time, and, having accomplished the first, proceeds to a second, so I should have, I hoped, the encouraging pleasure of seeing on my pages the progress I made in virtue, by clearing successively my lines of their spots, till in the end, by a number of courses, I should be happy in viewing a clean book, after a thirteen weeks' daily examination.

This my little book had for its motto these lines from Addison's *Cato:*

Here will I hold. If there's a power above us
(And that there is, all nature cries aloud
Through all her works), He must delight in virtue;
And that which He delights in must be happy.

Another from Cicero,

O vitae Philosophia dux! O virtutum indagatrix expultrixque vitiorum! Unus dies, bene et ex praeceptis tuis actus, peccanti immortalitati est antiponendus.

Another from the Proverbs of Solomon, speaking of wisdom or virtue:

"Length of days is in her right hand, and in her left hand riches and honor. Her ways are ways of pleasantness, and all her paths are peace."—iii. 16, 17.

And conceiving God to be the fountain of wisdom, I thought it right and necessary to solicit His assistance for obtaining it; to this end I formed the following little prayer, which was prefixed to my tables of examination, for daily use.

O powerful Goodness! bountiful Father! merciful Guide! Increase in me that wisdom which discovers my truest interest. Strengthen my resolutions to perform what that wisdom dictates. Accept my kind offices to Thy other children as the only return in my power for Thy continual favors to me.

I used also sometimes a little prayer which I took from Thomson's *Poems,* viz.:

Father of light and life, thou Good Supreme!
O teach me what is good; teach me Thyself!
Save me from folly, vanity, and vice,

METHODS AND AGENCIES OF SELF-EDUCATION

From every low pursuit; and fill my soul
With knowledge, conscious peace, and virtue pure;
Sacred, substantial, never-fading bliss!

The precept of order requiring that every part of my business should have its allotted time, one page in my little book contained the following scheme of employment for the twenty-four hours of a natural day.

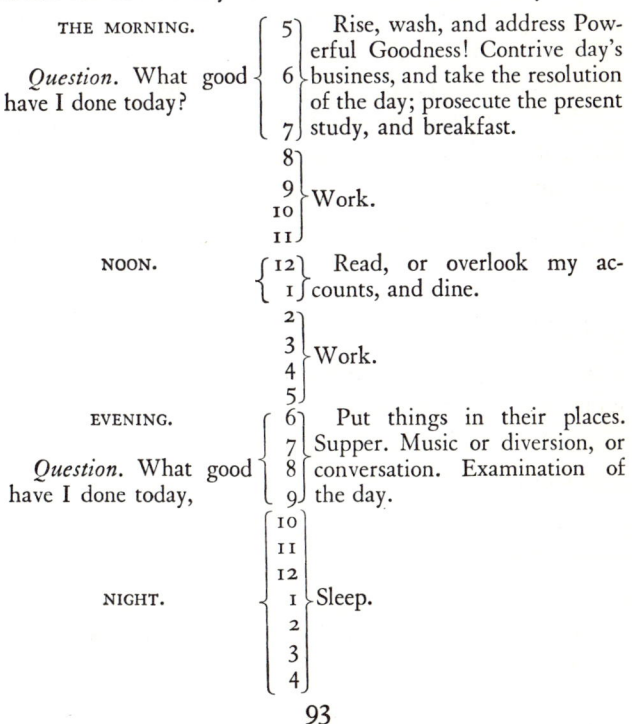

THE MORNING.	5	Rise, wash, and address Powerful Goodness! Contrive day's business, and take the resolution of the day; prosecute the present study, and breakfast.
Question. What good have I done today?	6	
	7	
	8	Work.
	9	
	10	
	11	
NOON.	12	Read, or overlook my accounts, and dine.
	1	
	2	Work.
	3	
	4	
	5	
EVENING.	6	Put things in their places. Supper. Music or diversion, or conversation. Examination of the day.
Question. What good have I done today,	7	
	8	
	9	
	10	Sleep.
	11	
	12	
NIGHT.	1	
	2	
	3	
	4	

I entered upon the execution of this plan for self-examination, and continued it with occasional intermissions for some time. I was surprised to find myself so much fuller of faults than I had imagined; but I had the satisfaction of seeing them diminish. To avoid the trouble of renewing now and then my little book, which, by scraping out the marks on the paper of old faults to make room for new ones in a new course, became full of holes, I transferred my tables and precepts to the ivory leaves of a memorandum book, on which the lines were drawn with red ink, that made a durable stain, and on those lines I marked my faults with a black-lead pencil, which marks I could easily wipe out with a wet sponge. After a while I went through one course only in a year, and afterward only one in several years, till at length I omitted them entirely, being employed in voyages and business abroad, with a multiplicity of affairs that interfered; but I always carried my little book with me.[16]

V

As his concern for moral well-being led him to adopt a self-rating scheme, so his concern for health resulted

---

[16] BIGELOW, JOHN, *The Works of Benjamin Franklin,* Vol. I, pp. 188–197. (By permission of G. P. Putnam's Sons, publishers, New York, 1904.)

METHODS AND AGENCIES OF SELF-EDUCATION

in a set of "Rules for Health and Long Life," published in *Poor Richard's Almanac,* 1742. Early in life, his thoughts had been turned to simplicity: first, by the example of his father's table; second, by a book by Tryon which gave many hints for simple, healthy living and especially recommended a vegetable diet; and, third, by the circumstances of the early years when he was struggling to get a foothold in the business world, which caused him to see the value of economies that not only released money for other purposes but also acted as a safeguard to health. Throughout life he was interested in health remedies that promised to make life more pleasant and useful. One of the questions always before the Junto was, "Have you or any of your acquaintances been lately sick or wounded? If so, what remedies were used, and what were their effects?"

Concern for comfort and health stimulated Franklin's interest in improving heating systems, eventually leading to the invention of the Pennsylvania fireplace. Through his energy and initiative in gaining subscriptions and the public support of the Pennsylvania Assembly, the Pennsylvania Hospital was founded, 1755.

FRANKLIN'S EDUCATIONAL VIEWS

He was also an enthusiastic advocate of bathing, using both the water and the air bath. Inoculation against smallpox found in him a warm champion, in a day when it was often opposed vigorously by medical men as well as others. The subject of common colds, too, occupied his mind for years during which he collected notes and records of observations he intended to use in publishing a paper on the subject. To go into his refutation of the charges against inoculation, his arguments concerning the contraction of colds, or the reasons for, and the benefits of, air bathing would lead us into a purely technical matter which cannot be dealt with here.

His popular message, to friends and the public generally, dealt chiefly with exercise and restraint of appetite. Franklin himself, in early life, was very active and became an expert swimmer. On one occasion, when in England, he swam from near Chelsea to Blackfryar's, nearly four miles and performed ". . . many feats of activity, both upon and under water, that surprised and pleased . . ." those with him. Later, he was offered the opportunity of teaching the sons of Sir William Wyndham to swim, and even considered setting up as a teacher of swimming in the city of London; but, arrangements having been partially concluded to return to Philadelphia in a business connection, the career of swimming instructor was closed to him. Those who constantly think of Franklin the philosopher may be intrigued with the following experience of July 25, 1785, so strange that he, too, would hardly have believed it possible.

"The Bishop and family lodging in the same inn, the Star, we all breakfast and dine together. I went at noon to bathe in Martin's salt-water hot-bath, and, floating on my back, fell asleep, and slept near an hour by my watch without sinking or turning! a thing I never did before, and should hardly have thought possible. Water is the easiest bed that can be." [17]

Having been vigorous in youth, and accustomed to heavy work in the printing shop—even wheeling his

[17] From Smyth, A. H., *The Writings of Benjamin Franklin,* Vol. X, p. 469. (By permission of The Macmillan Company, publishers, New York, 1905.)

own paper stock, occasionally, in Philadelphia—he suffered much from lack of it when diplomatic duties of the last two decades of life kept him much indoors. In 1767, he wrote to Debby, ". . . I begin to find a little giddiness in my head, a token that I want the exercise I have yearly been accustomed to . . ."[18] Again he said, in the *Craven Street Gazette* (1770), ". . . Dr. Fatsides made four hundred and sixty-nine turns in his dining-room . . ."; but it appears that exercise indoors was of little benefit to him. In the "Dialogue between Franklin and the Gout," written while at Passy, near Paris, he made clear that he recognized the disease as a result of improper eating and a lack of proper exercise. The days of simplicity were far in the past; and the words of Poor Richard little more than a memory. "To lengthen thy life," said Richard, "lessen thy meals." "Eat few suppers and you'll need few medicines." "Dine with little, sup with less, do better still, sleep supperless."

The following dietary regulations were published in *Poor Richard's Almanac,* 1742:

[18] *Ibid.,* Vol. V, p. 39.

METHODS AND AGENCIES OF SELF-EDUCATION

Rules of Health and Long Life

Eat and drink such an exact quantity as the constitution of thy body allows of, in reference to the services of the mind.

They that study much, ought not to eat so much as those that work hard, their digestion being not so good.

The exact quantity and quality, being found out, is to be kept to constantly.

Excess in all other things whatever, as well as in meat and drink, is also to be avoided.

Youth, age, and the sick, require a different quantity.

And so do those of contrary complexions; for that which is too much for a phlegmatic man, is not sufficient for a choleric.

The measure of food ought to be (as much as possibly may be) exactly proportionable to the quality and condition of the stomach, because the stomach digests it.

That quantity that is sufficient, the stomach can perfectly concoct and digest, and it sufficeth the due nourishment of the body.

A greater quantity of some things may be eaten than of others, some being of lighter digestion than others.

The difficulty lies in finding out an exact measure; but eat for necessity, not pleasure; for lust knows not where necessity ends.

FRANKLIN'S EDUCATIONAL VIEWS

Wouldst thou enjoy a long life, a healthy body, and a vigorous mind, and be acquainted also with the wonderful works of God, labor in the first place to bring thy appetite to reason.[19]

[19] SPARKS, JARED, *The Works of Benjamin Franklin*, Vol. II, pp. 86–87, Boston, 1836–1840.

CHAPTER III

FIRST STEPS OF A PRACTICAL EDUCATION

Comprising the text of "A Letter on the Temple of Learning" (1722); "Idea of the English School" (1751); Of the Education of Girls; and "A Petition of the Left Hand, to those Who Have the Superintendency of Education."

FRANKLIN's whole life bore testimony to the value he placed on practical things. His continual excursions into the unknown always had the purpose of bringing to light something useful to his fellow men. No study, not even a scientific one, should be pursued to the exclusion of other things of importance. No knowledge, he wrote, is equal, in importance and dignity, "with that of being a good parent, a good child, a good husband or wife, a good neighbor or friend, a good subject or citizen, that is, in short, a good Christian." [1] To "neglect

---

[1] Letter to Mary Hewson, June 11, 1760. From A. H. SMYTH, *The Writings of Benjamin Franklin,* Vol. IV, p. 22. (By permission of The Macmillan Company, publishers, New York, 1905.)

FRANKLIN'S EDUCATIONAL VIEWS

the knowledge and practice of essential duties" for the purpose of attaining eminence in a knowledge of nature is reprehensible. The question will be sure to cross the reader's mind, was it because he was writing to a woman that he advised putting practical duties ahead of scientific studies? To this one must answer, first, that, for that day, Franklin's ideas of women's education were fairly liberal, shaped, somewhat, by Defoe's, no doubt, although he believed it best for women not to enter into political disputes. Franklin, himself, moreover, though often lamenting the lack of leisure for philosophy, repeatedly put his scientific interests aside when called on for public service. This practice of putting duties first seems an indisputable answer.

Franklin's first step to a practical education was to avoid existing educational institutions, where nothing practical could be obtained. His contempt for the usual college education of his day was complete. The first step towards improving the situation was a critical, destructive one. Among his earliest literary ventures, at the age of sixteen, one finds forthright condemnation of the college, dominated as it was by wealth, ecclesiasticism, and useless ancient tongues. In his *Idea of the*

FIRST STEPS OF A PRACTICAL EDUCATION

English School, was recommended that practical education which should replace the rhyming verbiage of the collegians. When, in one of the Dogood letters, he gave a receipt for making a New England elegy, he did not miss the opportunity to say, mix ". . . all these ingredients well, put them into the empty skull of some young Harvard . . . and if you can procure a scrap of good Latin to put at the end . . . you will have an excellent elegy." The sharpest criticism appeared, however, in a letter published May, 7 to 14, 1722, wherein Silence reported her conversation with *Clericus,* her reverend boarder, and her dream of the Temple of Learning.

A Letter on the Temple of Learning

To the Author of The New England Courant [2]

SIR,

Discoursing the other day at dinner with my reverend boarder, formerly mentioned, (whom for distinction sake we will call by the name of *Clericus,*) concerning the education of children, I asked his advice about my young son William, whether or no I had best bestow

[2] From SMYTH, A. H., *The Writings of Benjamin Franklin,* Vol. II, pp. 9–14. (By permission of The Macmillan Company, publishers, New York, 1905.)

upon him academical learning, or (as our phrase is) bring him up at our college: He persuaded me to do it by all means, using many weighty arguments with me, and answering all the objections that I could form against it; telling me withal, that he did not doubt but that the lad would take his learning very well, and not idle away his time as too many there nowadays do. These words of *Clericus* gave me a curiosity to inquire a little more strictly into the present circumstances of that famous seminary of learning; but the information which he gave me, was neither pleasant, nor such as I expected.

As soon as dinner was over, I took a solitary walk into my orchard, still ruminating on *Clericus's* discourse with much consideration, until I came to my usual place of retirement under the Great Apple Tree; where having seated myself, and carelessly laid my head on a verdant bank, I fell by degrees into a soft and undisturbed slumber. My waking thoughts remained with me in my sleep, and before I awaked again, I dreamed the following dream.

I fancied I was traveling over pleasant and delightful fields and meadows, and through many small country towns and villages; and as I passed along all places resounded with the fame of the Temple of Learning: Every peasant, who had wherewithal, was preparing to

FIRST STEPS OF A PRACTICAL EDUCATION

send one of his children at least to this famous place; and in this case most of them consulted their own purses instead of their children's capacities: So that I observed, a great many, yea, the most part of those who were traveling thither, were little better than dunces and blockheads. Alas! Alas!

At length I entered upon a spacious plain, in the midst of which was erected a large and stately edifice: It was to this that a great company of youths from all parts of the country were going; so stepping in among the crowd, I passed on with them, and presently arrived at the gate.

The passage was kept by two sturdy porters named Riches and Poverty, and the latter obstinately refused to give entrance to any who had not first gained the favor of the former; so that I observed, many who came even to the very gate, were obliged to travel back again as ignorant as they came, for want of this necessary qualification. However, as a spectator I gained admittance, and with the rest entered directly into the temple.

In the middle of the great hall stood a stately and magnificent throne, which was ascended to by two high and difficult steps. On the top of it sat Learning in awful state; she was appareled wholly in black, and surrounded almost on every side with innumerable volumes in all languages. She seemed very busily employed in writing something on half a sheet of paper, and upon enquiry, I understood she was preparing a paper, called, *The New England Courant*. On her right hand sat English, with a pleasant smiling countenance, and handsomely attired; and on her left were seated several antique figures with their faces veiled. I was considerably puzzled to guess who they were, until one informed me, (who stood beside me,) that those figures on her left hand were Latin, Greek, Hebrew, etc., and that they were very much reserved, and seldom or never unveiled their faces here, and then to few or none, though most of those who have in this place acquired so much learning as to distinguish them from English, pretended to an intimate acquaintance with them. I then enquired of him, what could be the reason why they continued veiled, in this place especially: He pointed to the foot of the throne, where I saw Idleness, attended with Ignorance, and these (he informed me) were they, who first veiled them, and still kept them so.

Now I observed, that the whole tribe who entered into the temple with me, began to climb the throne; but the work proving troublesome and difficult to most of them, they withdrew their hands from the plow, and contented themselves to sit at the foot, with Madam Idleness and her Maid Ignorance, until those who were assisted by diligence and a docible temper, had well nigh

FIRST STEPS OF A PRACTICAL EDUCATION

got up the first step: But the time drawing nigh in which they could no way avoid ascending, they were fain to crave the assistance of those who had got before them, and who, for the reward perhaps of a pint of milk, or a piece of plum-cake, lent the lubbers a helping hand, and sat them in the eye of the world, upon a level with themselves.

The other step being in the same manner ascended, and the usual ceremonies at an end, every beetle-skull seemed well satisfied with his own portion of learning, though perhaps he was even just as ignorant as ever. And now the time of their departure being come, they marched out of doors to make room for another company, who waited for entrance: And I, having seen all that was to be seen, quitted the hall likewise, and went to make my observations on those who were just gone out before me.

Some I perceived took to merchandising, others to traveling, some to one thing, some to another, and some to nothing; and many of them from henceforth, for want of patrimony, lived as poor as church mice, being unable to dig, and ashamed to beg, and to live by their wits it was impossible. But the most part of the crowd went along a large beaten path, which led to a Temple at the further end of the plain, called, The Temple of Theology. The business of those who were employed in this Temple being laborious and painful, I wondered exceedingly to see so many go towards it; but while I was pondering this matter in my mind, I spied *Pecunia* behind a curtain, beckoning to them with her hand, which sight immediately satisfied me for whose sake it was, that a great part of them (I will not say all) traveled that road. In this Temple I saw nothing worth mentioning, except the ambitious and fraudulent contrivances of Plagius, who (notwithstanding he had been severely reprehended for such practices before) was diligently transcribing some eloquent paragraphs out of Tillotson's Works, etc., to embellish his own.

Now I bethought myself in my sleep, that it was time to be at home, and as I fancied I was traveling back thither, I reflected in my mind on the extreme folly of those parents, who, blind to their children's dullness, and insensible of the solidity of their skulls, because they think their purses can afford it, will needs send them to the Temple of Learning, where, for want of a suitable genius, they learn little more than how to carry themselves handsomely, and enter a room genteelly, (which might as well be acquired at a dancing school,) and from whence they return, after abundance of trouble and charge, as great blockheads as ever, only more proud and self-conceited.

FIRST STEPS OF A PRACTICAL EDUCATION

While I was in the midst of these unpleasant reflections, *Clericus* (who with a book in his hand was walking under the trees) accidentally awaked me; to him I related my dream with all its particulars, and he, without much study, presently interpreted it, assuring me, that it was a lively representation of HARVARD COLLEGE, et cetera.

> I remain, Sir,
> Your Humble Servant,
> SILENCE DOGOOD.

II

It appeared to Franklin inconceivably foolish to educate youth for places in life to which they would not be called. Every word of his educational projects, every practical agency of self and adult education which he founded, had its origin in this principle of practicality. To Richard Bache, who inquired about sending a second son, William, to France for an education, he wrote: ". . . I think a foreign education for one of your sons sufficient . . . I wish him however to learn French . . . Besides other usual things let him acquire a little mathematics, and a perfect knowledge of accounts.

With these he will be able to bustle and make his way." [3]

The utilitarian *raison d'être* of education, that made such a strong appeal to Franklin, is probably nowhere more pointedly and briefly put than in the story of the Indian chief's reply to the English commissioners, which he related, with evident approval, in a letter to Richard Jackson:

"The little value Indians set on what we prize so highly, under the name of learning, appears from a pleasant passage that happened some years since, at a treaty between some colonies and the Six Nations. When everything had been settled to the satisfaction of both sides, and nothing remained but a mutual exchange of civilities, the English Commissioners told the Indians that they had in their country a college for the instruction of youth, who were there taught various languages, arts, and sciences; that there was a particular foundation in favor of the Indians to defray the expense of the education of any of their sons, who should desire to take the benefit of it; and said, if the Indians would accept the offer, the English would take half a dozen of

[3] Letter to Richard Bache, Sept. 13, 1781. *Ibid.*, Vol. VIII, p. 305. (By permission of The Macmilian Company, publishers, New York, 1905.)

FIRST STEPS OF A PRACTICAL EDUCATION

their brightest lads, and bring them up in the best manner. The Indians, after consulting on the proposals, replied, that it was remembered that some of their youths had formerly been educated at that college, but that it had been observed that for a long time after they returned to their friends, *they were absolutely good for nothing;* being neither acquainted with the true methods of killing deer, catching beavers, or surprising an enemy. The proposition they looked on, however, as a mark of kindness and good will of the English to the Indian nations, which merited a grateful return; and therefore, if the English gentlemen would send a dozen or two of their children to Opondago, the Great Council would take care of their education, bring them up in what was really the best manner, and make men of them." [4]

Several manuscripts, prepared by Franklin, dealt specifically with the subject of English education as the most practical and immediately useful feature of the youth's preparation for everyday life. Franklin was also convinced of the political need for emphasis on English education in Pennsylvania, fearing that without the

[4] May 5, 1753. *Ibid.,* Vol. III, pp. 138–139. (By permission of The Macmillan Company, publishers, New York, 1905.)

FRANKLIN'S EDUCATIONAL VIEWS

establishment of English schools among the Germans, it would be impossible to "preserve our language, and even our government will become precarious." Here again the practical reason, which always stood back of his projects, is apparent. He was associated with the movement to establish charity schools for the minority group, furthered by the Society for Propagating the Knowledge of God among the Germans, which was assisted by the S. P. G. The three motives in this work —education, religion, and politics—appear to have been considerably mixed. The more prominent German sects accepted it as pure educational philanthropy at first, though minor sectarians were skeptical. Later, all became so. It is difficult, even now, to say, with finality, which of them was the most important purpose. But when one considers the views of Franklin and Smith, provost of the College in Philadelphia, and the great influence that both of them exercised, it is perfectly clear that the political motive was an active ferment in the movement. Franklin wrote to Richard Jackson, May 5, 1753, setting forth his idea as to the problem the Germans presented to the Colony and made clear his conception of education as an agency of social control.

FIRST STEPS OF A PRACTICAL EDUCATION

"I am perfectly of your mind, that measures of great temper are necessary with the Germans; and am not without apprehensions, that, through their indiscretion, or ours, or both, great disorders may one day arise among us. Those who come hither are generally of the most ignorant stupid sort of their own nation, and, as ignorance is often attended with credulity when knavery would mislead it, and with suspicion when honesty would set it right; and as few of the English understand the German language, and so cannot address them either from the press or pulpit, it is almost impossible to remove any prejudices they may entertain. Their own clergy have very little influence over their people, who seem to take an uncommon pleasure in abusing and discharging the minister on every trivial occasion. Not being used to liberty, they know not how to make a modest use of it. And as Kolben in his History says of the young Hottentots, that they are not esteemed men until they have shown their manhood by beating their mothers, so these seem not to think themselves free, till they can feel their liberty in abusing and insulting their teachers. Thus they are under no restraint from ecclesiastical government; they behave, however, submissively enough at present to the civil government, which I wish they may continue to do, for I remember when they modestly declined intermeddling in our elections, but now they come in droves and carry all before them, except in one or two counties.

"Few of their children in the country learn English. They import many books from Germany; and of the six printing-houses in the province, two are entirely German, two half-German half-English, and but two entirely English. They have one German newspaper, and one half-German. Advertisements, intended to be general, are now printed in Dutch and English. The signs in our streets have inscriptions in both languages, and in some places only German. They begin of late to make all their bonds and other legal instruments in their own language, which (though I think it ought not to be) are allowed good in our courts, where the German business so increases, that there is continued need of interpreters; and I suppose in a few years they will also be necessary in the Assembly, to tell one half of our legislators what the other half say.

"In short, unless the stream of their importation could be turned from this to other colonies, as you very judiciously propose, they will soon so outnumber us, that all the advantages we have, will not in my opinion be able to preserve our language, and even our government will become precarious. . . . Yet I am not entirely for refusing to admit them into our colonies. All that seems to me necessary is, to distribute them more

FIRST STEPS OF A PRACTICAL EDUCATION

equally, mix them with the English, establish English schools, where they are now too thick settled; and take some care to prevent the practice, lately fallen into by some of the ship-owners of sweeping the German gaols to make up the number of their passengers. I say, I am not against the admission of Germans in general, for they have their virtues. Their industry and frugality are exemplary. They are excellent husbandmen; and contribute greatly to the improvement of a country." [5]

Still another attempt was made by Franklin to fix practice into new moulds. To have effected a movement to create a new type of secondary school and college was perhaps his greatest single educational contribution, so far as institutional education is concerned. But, besides that, he harbored the idea of improving the content of studies and actually presented his proposals for a reformed system of spelling the English tongue (1768). As the system was never quite completed, probably because of his preoccupation with other affairs, it had no practical effect. Franklin wrote only a few letters, as examples, making use of the system and gave

[5] *Ibid.*, pp. 139–141. (By permission of The Macmillan Company, publishers, New York, 1905.)

FRANKLIN'S EDUCATIONAL VIEWS

his manuscript and types to Noah Webster, requesting that he should undertake the task of bringing about the practical reform. "Whether this project, so deeply interesting to this country," wrote Webster, in his *Dissertations on the English Language,* "will ever be effected; or whether it will be defeated by insolence and prejudice, remains for my countrymen to determine." [6]

Franklin never wrote an entire treatise during his whole lifetime; but he dashed off letters, plans, proposals, and projects, dealing with one phase or another of education, with the true insight of genius, whenever the time seemed propitious. Generally, in so doing, he was careful to let it appear that he was but modestly putting forward some project in behalf of friends, rather than that he was the author of it. He says, specifically, that he found this a useful method.

When he first drew up a plan for the Academy in Philadelphia, Franklin was, of course, strongly inclined to emphasize English education. He wrote, in "Obser-

---

[6] The text of *A Scheme for a New Alphabet and Reformed Mode of Spelling* and the examples of it, in letters, are given in A. H. SMYTH, *The Writings of Benjamin Franklin,* Vol. V, pp. 169–178. (The Macmillan Company, New York, 1905.)

FIRST STEPS OF A PRACTICAL EDUCATION

vations Relative to the Intentions of the Original Founders of the Academy":

". . . my ideas went no further than to procure the means of a good English education. A number of my friends, to whom I communicated the proposal, concurred with me in these ideas; but Mr. Allen, Mr. Francis, Mr. Peters, and some other persons of wealth and learning, whose subscriptions and countenance we should need, being of opinion that it ought to include the learned languages, I submitted my judgment to theirs, retaining however a strong prepossession in favor of my first plan, and resolving to preserve as much of it as I could, and to nourish the English school by every means in my power."[7]

Thus, it appears that Franklin, hearkening to the voice of expediency, on the part of his friends, included education in the classics and other studies but did not give up his own preference. Later, in the same exposition of the trustees' failure to live up to the original intentions of the founders, he said:

"I wrote also a paper, entitled *Idea of the English School,* which was printed, and afterwards annexed to

[7] SPARKS, JARED, *The Works of Benjamin Franklin,* Vol. II, pp. 133–134, Boston, 1836–1840.

Mr. Peters' sermon, preached at the opening of the Academy. This paper was said to be for the consideration of the trustees; and the expectation of the public, that the idea might in a great measure be carried into execution, contributed to render the subscriptions more liberal as well as more general." [8]

The *Idea of the English School* expressed Franklin's most cherished belief in, and most definite formulation of, an institution for vernacular training. Whatever may have been accomplished at the Academy, later, we may learn from this document what Franklin thought should be the first business of education.

A copy of his "Idea" was sent to Samuel Johnson who replied, in part, as follows, expressing great approval of it and surprise at the completeness and soundness of the proposal:

"Nobody would imagine that the draught you have made for an English education was done by a tradesman. But so it sometimes is, a true genius will not content itself without entering more or less into almost everything, and of mastering many things more in spite of fate itself. I cannot pretend to be qualified to criticize much on things of this kind having never

[8] *Ibid.*, pp. 137–139.

FIRST STEPS OF A PRACTICAL EDUCATION

had anything that could be called an education myself, the most of what I did learn being of such a cobweb kind that the best thing I could do with it was to forget it as fast as I could. So that I am free to say that I am not able to find any fault with your scheme much less to devise a better. So far from this that I can't but admire it as a most excellent draught and particularly your contrivance to promote [public?] speaking and sundry observations on the advantages of good reading and speaking. The only thing I can think of that may meliorate what you have done is that as the business of your third class seems less than that of the others, and that you say nothing of rhetoric and oratory considered as an art, perhaps you might have done well to prescribe in that year the learning of some system of rhetoric so as to have a good notion of the tropes and figures. The best I know of is that of Blackwell on the classics; this therefore and the Port Royal art of speaking . . . would be well thumbed in that year. And . . . you might do well to mention Milton and Telemachus and the Travels of Cyrus with the works of Shakespeare, Addison and Pope and Swift . . . as the best English classics." [9]

[9] Letter of Samuel Johnson to Benjamin Franklin. From A. H. SMYTH, *The Writings of Benjamin Franklin,* Vol. III, pp. 29-30. (By permission of The Macmillan Company, publishers, New York, 1905.)

FRANKLIN'S EDUCATIONAL VIEWS

Idea of the English School

Sketched out for the consideration of the Trustees of the Philadelphia Academy

It is expected that every scholar to be admitted into this school be at least able to pronounce and divide the syllables in reading, and to write a legible hand. None to be received that are under —[10] years of age.

First or Lowest Class

Let the First Class learn the English grammar rules, and at the same time let particular care be taken to improve them in orthography. Perhaps the latter is best done by pairing the scholars, two of those nearest equal in their spelling to be put together; let these strive for victory, each propounding ten words every day to the other to be spelt. He that spells truly most of the other's words is victor for that day; he that is victor most days in a month, to obtain a prize, a pretty neat book of some kind useful in their future studies. This method fixes the attention of children extremely to the orthography of words, and makes them good spellers very

---

[10] This is blank in the original. D. E. Cloyd, *Franklin and Education,* inserted "nine." Franklin, in a letter to Samuel Johnson dated Oct. 25, 1750, said he supposed the boys to be between eight and sixteen years of age.

early. 'Tis a shame for a man to be so ignorant of this little art, in his own language, as to be perpetually confounding words of like sound and different significations; the consciousness of which defect makes some men, otherwise of good learning and understanding, averse to writing even a common letter.

Let the pieces read by the scholars in this class be short, such as Croxall's *Fables,* and little stories. In giving the lesson, let it be read to them; let the meaning of the difficult words in it be explained to them, and let them con it over by themselves before they are called to read to the master, or usher, who is to take particular care that they do not read too fast and that they duly observe the stops and pauses. A vocabulary of the most usual difficult words might be formed for their use, with explanations; and they might daily get a few of those words and explanations by heart, which would a little exercise their memories; or at least they might write a number of them in a small book for the purpose, which would help to fix the meaning of those words in their minds, and at the same time furnish every one with a little dictionary for his future use.

The Second Class to be taught

Reading with attention and with proper modulations of the voice according to the sentiments and subject.

FRANKLIN'S EDUCATIONAL VIEWS

Some short pieces, not exceeding the length of a *Spectator,* to be given this class as lessons (and some of the easier *Spectators* would be very suitable for the purpose). These lessons might be given over night as tasks, the scholars to study them against the morning. Let it then be required of them to give an account, first of the parts of speech and construction of one or two sentences; this will oblige them to recur frequently to their grammar, and fix its principal rules in their memory. Next of the intention of the writer, or the scope of the piece; the meaning of each sentence, and of every uncommon word. This would early acquaint them with the meaning and force of words, and give them that most necessary habit of reading with attention.

The master then to read the piece with the proper modulations of voice, due emphasis, and suitable action, where action is required; and put the youth on imitating his manner. Where the author has used an expression not the best, let it be pointed out; and let his beauties be particularly remarked to the youth.

Let the lessons for reading be varied, that the youth may be made acquainted with good styles of all kinds in prose and verse, and the proper manner of reading each kind. Sometimes a well-told story, a piece of a sermon, a general's speech to his soldiers, a speech in a

FIRST STEPS OF A PRACTICAL EDUCATION

tragedy, some part of a comedy, an ode, a satire, a letter, blank verse, Hudibrastic, heroic, etc. But let such lessons for reading be chosen as contain some useful instruction, whereby the understandings or morals of the youth may at the same time be improved.

It is required that they should first study and understand the lessons before they are put upon reading them properly, to which end each boy should have an English dictionary to help him over difficulties. When our boys read English to us we are apt to imagine they understand what they read because we do, and because 'tis their mother tongue. But they often read as parrots speak, knowing little or nothing of the meaning. And it is impossible a reader should give the due modulation to his voice, and pronounce properly, unless his understanding goes before his tongue and makes him master of the sentiment. Accustoming boys to read aloud what they do not first understand is the cause of those even-set tones so common among readers, which when they have once got a habit of using they find so difficult to correct; by which means among fifty readers we scarcely find a good one. For want of good reading, pieces published with a view to influence the minds of men for their own or the public benefit lose half their force. Were there but one good reader in a neighborhood a public orator might be heard throughout a nation with the same advantages, and have the same effect on his audience, as if they stood within the reach of his voice.

The Third Class to be taught

Speaking properly and gracefully, which is near of kin to good reading and naturally follows it in the studies of youth. Let the scholars of this class begin with learning the elements of rhetoric from some short system, so as to be able to give an account of the most usual tropes and figures. Let all their bad habits of speaking, all offences against good grammar, all corrupt or foreign accents, and all improper phrases, be pointed out to them. Short speeches from the Roman or other history, or from our parliamentary debates, might be got by heart and delivered with the proper action, etc. Speeches and scenes in our best tragedies and comedies (avoiding everything that could injure the morals of youth) might likewise be got by rote, and the boys exercised in delivering or acting them; great care being taken to form their manner after the truest models.

For their farther improvement, and a little to vary their studies, let them now begin to read history, after having got by heart a short table of the principal epochs

FIRST STEPS OF A PRACTICAL EDUCATION

in chronology. They may begin with Rollin's ancient and Roman histories and proceed at proper hours as they go through the subsequent classes, with the best histories of our own nation and colonies. Let emulation be excited among the boys by giving, weekly, little prizes or other small encouragements to those who are able to give the best account of what they have read, as to times, places, names of persons, etc. This will make them read with attention, and imprint the history well in their memories. In remarking on the history the master will have fine opportunities of instilling instruction of various kinds, and improving the morals as well as the understandings of youth.

The natural and mechanic history contained in [the] *Spectacle de la Nature* might also be begun in this class, and continued through the subsequent classes by other books of the same kind; for next to the knowledge of duty, this kind of knowledge is certainly the most useful, as well as the most entertaining. The merchant may thereby be enabled better to understand many commodities in trade; the handicraftsman to improve his business by new instruments, mixtures and materials; and frequently hints are given of new manufactures, or new methods of improving land, that may be set on foot greatly to the advantage of a country.

The Fourth Class to be Taught

Composition. Writing one's own language well is the next necessary accomplishment after good speaking. 'Tis the writing master's business to take care that the boys make fair characters, and place them straight and even in the lines; but to form their style, and even to take care that the stops and capitals are properly disposed, is the part of the English master. The boys should be put on writing letters to each other on any common occurrences, and on various subjects, imaginary business, etc., containing little stories, accounts of their late reading, what parts of authors please them and why. Letters of congratulation, of compliment, of request, of thanks, of recommendation, of admonition, of consolation, of expostulation, excuse, etc. In these they should be taught to express themselves clearly, concisely, and naturally, without affected words or high-flown phrases. All their letters to pass through the master's hand, who is to point out the faults, advise the corrections, and commend what he finds right. Some of the best letters published in our own language, as Sir William Temple's, those of Pope and his friends, and some others, might be set before the youth as models, their beauties pointed out and explained by the master, the letters themselves transcribed by the scholar.

Dr. Johnson's *Ethices Elementa,* or First Principles of Morality, may now be read by the scholars and explained by the master, to lay a solid foundation of virtue and piety in their minds. And as this class continues the reading of history let them now at proper hours receive some farther instructions in chronology, and in that part of geography (from the mathematical master) which is necessary to understand the maps and globes. They should also be acquainted with the modern names of the places they find mentioned in ancient writers. The exercises of good reading and proper speaking still continued at suitable times.

Fifth Class

To improve the youth in composition they may now, besides continuing to write letters, begin to write little essays in prose; and sometimes in verse, not to make them poets, but for this reason, that nothing acquaints a lad so speedily with variety of expression as the necessity of finding such words and phrases as will suit with the measure, sound and rhyme of verse, and at the same time well express the sentiment. These essays should all pass under the master's eye, who will point out their faults and put the writer on correcting them. Where the judgment is not ripe enough for forming new essays, let the sentiments of a *Spectator* be given, and required to be clothed in a scholar's own words; or the circumstances of some good story, the scholar to find expression. Let them be put sometimes on abridging a paragraph of a diffuse author, sometimes on dilating or amplifying what is wrote more closely. And now let Dr. Johnson's *Noetica,* or First Principles of Human Knowledge, containing a Logic, or Art of Reasoning, etc., be read by the youth, and the difficulties that may occur to them be explained by the master. The reading of history and the exercises of good reading and just speaking still continued.

Sixth Class

In this class, besides continuing the studies of the preceding, in history, rhetoric, logic, moral and natural philosophy the best English authors may be read and explained; as Tillotson, Milton, Locke, Addison, Pope, Swift, the higher papers in the *Spectator* and *Guardian,* the best translations of Homer, Virgil and Horace, of Telemachus, Travels of Cyrus, etc.

Once a year, let there be public exercises in the hall, the trustees and citizens present. Then let fine gilt books be given as prizes to such boys as distinguish

FIRST STEPS OF A PRACTICAL EDUCATION

themselves and excel the others in any branch of learning; making three degrees of comparison, giving the best prize to him that performs best, a less valuable one to him that comes up next to the best, and another to the third. Commendations, encouragement and advice to the rest, keeping up their hopes that by industry they may excel another time. The names of those that obtain the prizes to be yearly printed in a list.

The hours of each day are to be divided and disposed in such a manner as that some classes may be with the writing master, improving their hands; others with the mathematical master, learning arithmetic, accounts, geography, use of the globes, drawing, mechanics, etc.; while the rest are in the English school, under the English master's care.

Thus instructed, youth will come out of this school fitted for learning any business, calling or profession, except such wherein languages are required; and though unacquainted with any ancient or foreign tongue, they will be masters of their own, which is of more immediate and general use; and withal will have attained many other valuable accomplishments; the time usually spent in acquiring those languages, often without success, being here employed in laying such a foundation of knowledge and ability as, properly improved, may qualify them to pass through and execute the several offices of civil life, with advantage and reputation to themselves and country.

B.F.[11]

III

A girl's life in Colonial days was a very practical affair. Franklin would not change it much, though he would improve its utility by practical education. Of the education of girls, Franklin wrote little; but his approving quotation from Defoe, in an early Dogood letter, indicates the trend of his thought. Mrs. Silence Dogood, herself, was narrowly educated ". . . in all that knowledge and learning which is necessary for our sex . . . ," was denied no accomplishment to be obtained in a country place, such as "all sorts of needlework, writing, arithmetic . . . ," and read "ingenious books" in the library of her master. But this description gives a rosier picture than was to be generally found in practice. In general, a practical and religious education, plus ac-

---

[11] Reprinted from William Kent Gilbert's *History of the College & Academy of Philadelphia* . . . Philadelphia, 1863. It was first printed as an appendix to "A Sermon on Education" (wherein some account is given of the Academy, established in the city of Philadelphia), preached by Reverend Richard Peters, Jan. 7, 1751.

FIRST STEPS OF A PRACTICAL EDUCATION

complishments, seemed to Franklin the ideal for a girl. Having been favorably impressed by the wife of a partner who handled his business well after his death, he was convinced that accounts offered a desirable preparation, in anticipation of that "melancholy state of widowhood."

"I mention this affair chiefly for the sake of recommending that branch of education for our young females, as likely to be of more use to them and their children, in case of widowhood, than either music or dancing, by preserving them from losses by imposition of crafty men and enabling them to continue, perhaps, a profitable mercantile house, with established correspondence till a son is grown up fit to undertake and go on with it, to the lasting advantage and enriching of the family." [12]

A number of his young women correspondents were encouraged in philosophical tendencies, but he urged on them "a prudent moderation" in that respect. To Debby he wrote recommending that Sally should ap-

[12] BIGELOW, JOHN, *The Works of Benjamin Franklin,* Vol. I, p. 210. (By permission of G. P. Putnam's Sons, publishers, New York, 1904.)

FRANKLIN'S EDUCATIONAL VIEWS

ply ". . . herself closely to her French and music . . ." and with a wish that she were ". . . a little more careful of her spelling . . ." Again, seven years later, he urged: "Let Sally divert you with her music. Put her on practising on the Armonica. . . ." Education was to prepare girls for a useful, pleasant domestic life. To Debby, his "Dear Child," he wrote with fatherly commendation, in 1758:

"You are very prudent not to engage in party disputes. Women never should meddle with them except in endeavors to reconcile their husbands, brothers, and friends, who happen to be of contrary sides. If your sex can keep cool, you may be a means of cooling ours the sooner, and restoring more speedily that social harmony among fellow-citizens, that is so desirable after long and bitter dissensions." [13]

Though Franklin thought profoundly about religion, he found it hard to go to church. This example did not appear to him good for his women folk to follow. To his daughter, Sally, he wrote, urging the contrary:

[13] From SMYTH, A. H., *The Writings of Benjamin Franklin*, Vol. III, p. 439. (By permission of The Macmillan Company, publishers, New York, 1905.)

FIRST STEPS OF A PRACTICAL EDUCATION

"Go constantly to church, whoever preaches. The act of devotion in the Common Prayer Book is your principal business there, and if properly attended to will do more toward amending the heart than sermons generally can do. For they were composed by men of much greater piety and wisdom than our common composers of sermons can pretend to be, and therefore I wish you would never miss the prayer days; yet I do not mean you should despise sermons, even of the preachers you dislike, for the discourse is often much better than a man, as sweet and clear waters come through very dirty earth. I am the more particular on this head, as you seemed to express a little before I came away some inclination to leave our church, which I would not have you do." [14]

IV

Among lighter essays, on a variety of subjects, written at uncertain dates, in Paris and London, probably partially as a diversion for his friends and himself, is found one which refers to the one-sided education of his day. Under the title, "A Petition of the Left Hand,

[14] BIGELOW, JOHN, *The Works of Benjamin Franklin,* Vol. IV, p. 20. (By permission of G. P. Putnam's Sons, publishers, New York, 1904.)

to Those Who Have the Superintendency of Education," he pointed out the pernicious effects of education which develops man in one direction and ignores his possibilities completely in another. This essay was first published, as one of the "Bagatelles," in William Temple Franklin's edition of Franklin's works, in 1818.

A Petition of the Left Hand to Those Who Have the Superintendency of Education

I address myself to all the friends of youth, and conjure them to direct their compassionate regards to my unhappy fate, in order to remove the prejudices of which I am the victim. There are twin sisters of us; and the two eyes of man do not more resemble, nor are capable of being upon better terms with each other, than my sister and myself, were it not for the partiality of our parents, who make the most injurious distinctions between us. From my infancy, I have been led to consider my sister as a being of more elevated rank. I was suffered to grow up without the least instruction, while nothing was spared in her education. She had masters to teach her writing, drawing, music, and other accomplishments; but if by chance I touched a pencil, a pen,

FIRST STEPS OF A PRACTICAL EDUCATION

or a needle, I was bitterly rebuked; and more than once I have been beaten for being awkward, and wanting a graceful manner. It is true, my sister associated me with her upon some occasions; but she always made a point of taking the lead, calling upon me only from necessity, or to figure by her side.

But conceive not, Sirs, that my complaints are instigated merely by vanity. No; my uneasiness is occasioned by an object much more serious. It is the practice in our family, that the whole business of providing for its subsistence falls upon my sister and myself. If any disposition should attack my sister,—and I mention it in confidence upon this occasion, that she is subject to the gout, the rheumatism, and cramp, without making mention of other accidents,—what would be the fate of our poor family? Must not the regret of our parents be excessive, at having placed so great a difference between sisters who are so perfectly equal? Alas! we must perish from distress; for it would not be in my power even to scrawl a suppliant petition for relief, having been obliged to employ the hand of another in transcribing the request which I have now the honor to prefer to you.

Condescend, Sirs, to make my parents sensible of the injustice of an exclusive tenderness, and of the necessity of distributing their care and affection among all their children equally. I am, with a profound respect, Sirs, your obedient servant,

THE LEFT HAND.[15]

[15] SPARKS, JARED, *The Works of Benjamin Franklin,* Vol. II, pp. 183–184, Boston, 1836–1840.

CHAPTER IV

FRANKLIN AND THE ACADEMY

Wherein are reprinted his "Proposals Relating to the Education of Youth in Pennsylvania" (1749); the "Constitutions of the Public Academy, in the City of Philadelphia"; "Observations Relative to the Intentions of the Original Founders of the Academy in Philadelphia" (1789); and an essay "On the Usefulness of the Mathematics" (1735).

I

WHEN the American Colonies were first planted on the Atlantic seaboard, educational fashions that had been followed for generations were brought along with the hardy colonists. The character of elementary, secondary, and higher education was but little changed during the first ten decades of colonial experience; but the attitude toward learning of the long-established pattern began to change and a new conception of education found warm adherents and advocates in the second half of the eighteenth century. In the field of what is today generally termed "secondary education," the founding fathers had the Latin Grammar School, which was encouraged by law (1647) in Massachusetts, whose example was here and there followed by others. At various places in the South, endowments were provided for schools similar in type, while in New Amsterdam efforts were made to found a Latin School, and in Pennsylvania the Quakers, pursuant to the educational policies of the Proprietary and their Society, founded the Penn Charter School under the direction of a board of overseers which also promoted elementary schools.

The purpose, written into the Law of 1647 by Massachusetts, of cheating "that old deluder, Satan," by causing men to be instructed in the tongues that learning might not be buried in the graves of the fathers may justly be considered true for other colonies. More specifically, these Latin schools aimed to prepare for colleges and the latter were created to prepare preachers in the principles of Calvinistic theology or bring them up to a knowledge of the true religion of the Church of England. This narrow professional purpose of the colleges—and except as ministers on occasion became teachers, they had no other—brought them under sharp criticism from the awakening middle class. Franklin,

FRANKLIN AND THE ACADEMY

while working on his brother's paper, *The New England Courant,* at the age of seventeen, was one among many bitter critics of the ecclesiastics. In one issue he declared, under the name of Silence Dogood, that rich men's sons went to college (Harvard) because they were rich; that they were often unable to mount the "throne of learning" and when it became difficult were content to sit at the feet of "Madam Idleness and her Maid Ignorance"; and that they were able to get their degrees only because they were rich enough to pay poorer ones for assistance.

That the colleges and their preparatory institutions were of a class character was borne in upon Josiah Franklin when he decided to send his favorite son, a mere child, to school. Seeing Benjamin had unusual talents, the father intended him for the ministry, the most respectable learned profession of the day. He continued at the grammar school less than one year, however, for, although he had made good progress, ". . . father, in the meantime, from a view of the expense of a college education, which having so large a family he could not well afford, and the mean living many so educated were afterwards able to obtain . . .

altered his first intention, [and] took me from the Grammar School. . . ." The private-school masters were at their job, however, giving utilitarian education, denied in the college preparatory schools. Franklin was sent to one of them, George Brownell. Later, in Philadelphia, he found them doing the same sort of thing. Some of the most famous in that city he was able to bring into the service of a newly organized institution, the Academy, which obtained a charter from the state and was regulated by a board of trustees.

In the *Autobiography,* Franklin relates his general satisfaction with his situation in Philadelphia. But two things, he lamented—the lack of any means of defense and the absence of provision "for a complete education of youth." The offering of the Penn Charter School he either discounted or overlooked altogether. As early as 1743, he drew up a proposal for an Academy and made advances to Reverend Peters to become head of it. Upon the latter's refusal, and other affairs distracting his attention, notably the trouble with Spain and France, the project was put aside until the coming of peace. Franklin described the launching of the *Proposals* (1749) as follows:

FRANKLIN AND THE ACADEMY

"Peace being concluded, and the association business therefore at an end, I turned my thoughts again to the affair of establishing an academy. The first step I took was to associate in the design a number of active friends, of whom the Junto furnished a good part; the next was to write and publish a pamphlet, entitled *Proposals Relating to the Education of Youth in Pennsylvania*. This I distributed among the principal inhabitants gratis; and as soon as I could suppose their minds a little prepared by the perusal of it, I set on foot a subscription for opening and supporting an academy; it was to be paid in quotas yearly for five years; by so dividing it, I judged the subscription might be larger and I believe it was so, amounting to no less, if I remember right, than five thousand pounds.

"In the introduction to these proposals, I stated their publication, not as an act of mine, but of some public-spirited gentlemen, avoiding as much as I could, according to my usual rule, the presenting myself to the public as the author of any scheme for their benefit.

"The subscribers, to carry the project into immediate execution, chose out of their number twenty-four trustees and appointed Mr. Francis, then attorney-general and myself to draw up constitutions for the government of the academy; which being done and signed, a house was hired, masters engaged, and the schools opened, I think, in the same year, 1749."[1]

The character of this new institution was to be utilitarian. Its purposes, to ". . . supply the succeeding age with men qualified to serve the public with honor to themselves, and to their country . . ." and to establish young men in business and other offices ". . . when they have behaved well and gone through their studies . . ." reveal the hand of the potter, the bourgeois Benjamin. If the Academy, thus launched, failed to live close to the principles of the mind which conceived it, the fault was not Franklin's (save as his long absences kept him apart from it), as is to be seen from a perusal of his "Observations Relative to the Intentions of the Original Founders."[2]

Besides the general purpose named above, the new institution was to serve in the preparation of teachers. Franklin always held the vocation of teaching in high

---

[1] BIGELOW, JOHN, *The Works of Benjamin Franklin,* Vol. I, pp. 238–239. (By permission of G. P. Putnam's Sons, publishers, New York, 1904.)

[2] See pp. 192–229.

regard. Writing to Dr. Samuel Johnson, Aug. 23, 1750, he gave judgment as to the social utility of education of youth, the profession of teaching.

"I think with you, that nothing is of more importance for the public weal, than to form and train up youth in wisdom and virtue. Wise and good men are, in my opinion, the strength of a state; much more so than riches or arms, which, under the management of ignorance and wickedness, often draw on destruction, instead of providing for the safety of the people. And though the culture bestowed on many should be successful only with a few, yet the influence of those few, and the service in their power may be very great. Even a single woman, that was wise, by her wisdom saved the city.

"I think also that general virtue is more probably to be expected and obtained from the education of youth, than from the exhortation of adult persons; bad habits and vices of the mind being, like diseases of the body, more easily prevented than cured. I think, moreover, that talents for the education of youth are the gift of God; and that he on whom they are bestowed, whenever a way is opened for the use of them, is as strongly called as if he heard a voice from heaven; nothing more surely

FRANKLIN'S EDUCATIONAL VIEWS

pointing out duty in a public service, than ability and opportunity of performing it." [3]

Elsewhere, he wrote, ". . . a number of the poorer sort will hereby be qualified to act as schoolmasters in the country." As a matter of fact, academies became the chief centers of teacher preparation in the United States, frequently having special classes or courses for this purpose, and thus continued until normal schools were created for this single end.

Franklin was one of the trustees and took a most active interest in the young institution until his death. The "Observations," wherein he sought to remind the trustees of their obligations, were written shortly before his death. In earlier years his letters were full of references to it, many concerning obtaining suitable masters. August 9, 1750, writing to Samuel Johnson, he encouraged him to accept "the management of the English Education" at a salary of £100 sterling, with charges of removal paid by the Trustees, the possibility of employing his son as a tutor at £60 or £70, and receipt of

[3] BIGELOW, JOHN, *The Works of Benjamin Franklin,* Vol. II, p. 320. (By permission of G. P. Putnam's Sons, publishers, New York, 1904.)

"something considerable yearly" from "marriages and christenings in the best families," as added inducements. He and the Trustees were thus anxious to secure a man ". . . whose experience and judgment would be of great use in forming rules and establishing good methods in the beginning, and whose name for learning would give it a reputation." He pointed out, further, that the Trustees were, three-fourths of them, members of the Church of England and "the rest men of moderate principles," that the city had voted £300 down and £100 a year to the Trustees; that £5,000 was already subscribed and that, as the Trustees were a self-perpetuating body, not subject to be changed by the caprice of a governor or the people, he foresaw a sound future for the infant institution.[4] Later, in 1750, he wrote Johnson of the smallpox epidemic, which blocked his coming; and sent a copy of his *Idea of the English School* for the Doctor's criticism. In 1751, the Academy was doing well, had excellent masters and seventy scholars. Three months later, it was "flourishing beyond expectation," had over one hundred

[4] SMYTH, A. H., *The Writings of Benjamin Franklin,* Vol. III, pp. 12–15. (The Macmillan Company, New York, 1905.)

scholars, and was "daily increasing," reported the delighted father. The Latin master received £200, the English, £150, the mathematics, £125, and three tutors, each £60.[5] Franklin's letters continued, for many years, to contain references to the Academy and College. In 1756, after its auspicious beginning, he lamented the decline in number of students and popularity under Smith and hoped he would give less time to politics in the future and more to his proper business.[6] Later he wrote, ". . . Smith continues still in the Academy; but I imagine will not much longer, unless he mends his manners greatly, for the schools decline on his account. . . ."[7]

Names and things have often been confused. Thus it is difficult to state exactly when the first academy arose. Since early in the eighteenth century, certain schools, called "academies," had come into being which, sometimes, had characteristics of the new realism which set them apart from the usual Latin schools. The "Academy" at Charleston, S. C. (1712), Tennent's Log

---

[5] *Ibid.,* pp. 53-54.
[6] *Ibid.,* p. 340.
[7] *Ibid.,* p. 353. (By permission of The Macmillan Company, publishers, New York, 1905.)

FRANKLIN AND THE ACADEMY

College of New Jersey, called by some an "academy," and numerous other schools so named, advertised in the Colonial newspapers before the middle of the century —all fall short, in some respects, of the true academy. The institution proposed by Franklin in 1743 and described in the published proposals in 1749 was a clearcut innovation, not only in name but in reality. He did not wish to create another Harvard. Franklin made clear its kinship to the foreign notion of realistic academies, as far as theory was concerned; and, in practice, the new school brought the practical studies, formerly taught only by adventure masters of the city, into the light of respectability and under the regulation of a board of trustees.

This essay, *Proposals Relating to the Education of Youth in Pennsylvania,* is reprinted as it was published by Franklin, in 1749, except that modern capitalization and spelling are followed. If Franklin can be said to have had one single purpose in life it was to do good to his fellow men and enjoy life at the same time. His *Proposals* were not original except in the sense that he brought novel views to the attention of many Pennsylvania readers and took practical measures to

FRANKLIN'S EDUCATIONAL VIEWS

create an institution about which many had written but done nothing. That his realistic notions were either (1) derived from others or (2) found their support in the arguments of other learned men is spread on every one of his pages. The notes, though cumbersome, are reprinted with his text, in order that students may understand his unity with, and the extent of his indebtedness to, other educational realists.

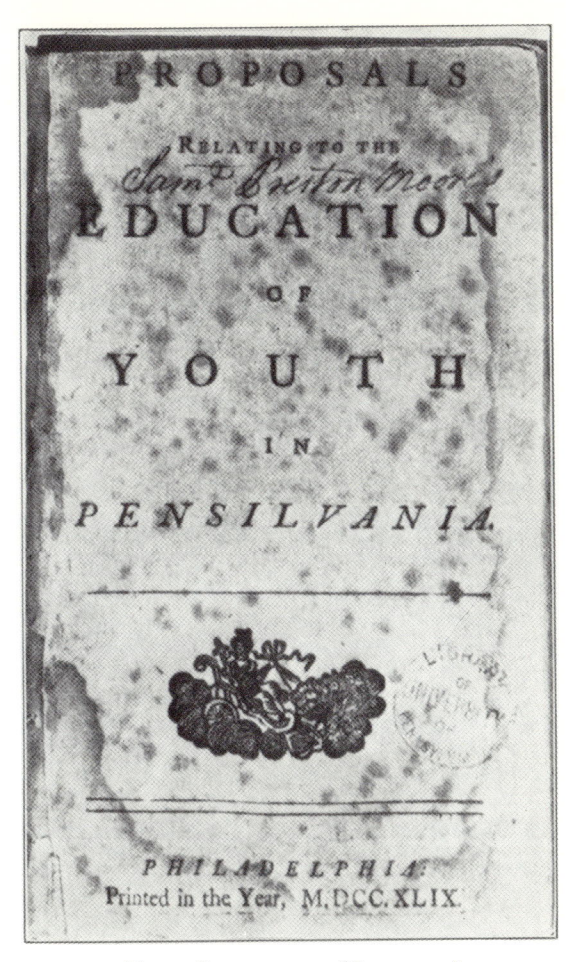

TITLE PAGE OF THE "PROPOSALS"

(*Facing page 148*)

ADVERTISEMENT TO THE READER

It has long been regretted as a misfortune to the youth of this Province, that we have no ACADEMY, in which they might receive the accomplishments of a regular education.

The following paper of hints towards forming a plan for that purpose, is so far approved by some public-spirited gentlemen, to whom it has been privately communicated, that they have directed a number of copies to be made by the press, and properly distributed, in order to obtain the sentiments and advice of men of learning, understanding, and experience in these matters; and have determined to use their interest and best endeavors, to have the scheme, when completed, carried gradually into execution; in which they have reason to believe they shall have the hearty concurrence and assistance of many who are well-wishers to their country.

Those who incline to favor the design with their advice, either as to the parts of learning to be taught, the order of study, the method of teaching, the economy of the school, or any other matter of importance to the success of the undertaking, are desired to communicate their sentiments as soon as may be, by letter directed to B. Franklin, Printer, in Philadelphia.[8]

[8] Reprinted from the original text, published at Philadelphia, 1749, in the Library of the University of Pennsylvania.

AUTHORS QUOTED IN THIS PAPER

1. The famous Milton, whose learning and abilities are well known, and who had practised some time the education of youth, so could speak from experience.

2. The great Mr. Locke, who wrote a treatise on education, well known, and much esteemed, being translated into most of the modern languages of Europe.

3. *Dialogues on Education,* 2 vols. Octavo, that are much esteemed, having had two editions in 3 years. Supposed to be wrote by the ingenious Mr. Hutcheson (author of *A Treatise on the Passions,* and another on the *Ideas of Beauty and Virtue*) who has had much experience in educating of youth, being a professor in the college at Glasgow, etc.

4. The learned Mr. Obadiah Walker, who had been many years a tutor to young noblemen, and wrote a treatise *On the Education of a Young Gentleman;* of which the fifth edition was printed 1687.

5. The much admired Mons. Rollin, whose whole life was spent in a college; and wrote 4 vols. on education, under the title of, *The Method of Teaching and Studying the Belles Lettres;* which are translated into English, Italian, and most of the modern languages.

6. The learned and ingenious Dr. George Turnbull, chaplain to the present Prince of Wales; who has had much experience in the educating of youth, and published a book, Octavo, entitled, **Observations on Liberal Education, in All Its Branches,** 1742.

With some others.

PROPOSALS, ETC.

The good education of youth has been esteemed by wise men in all ages, as the surest foundation of the happiness both of private families and of commonwealths. Almost all governments have therefore made it a principal object of their attention, to establish and endow with proper revenues, such seminaries of learning, as might supply the succeeding age with men qualified to serve the public with honor to themselves, and to their country.[9]

[9] As some things here proposed may be found to differ a little from the forms of education in common use, the following quotations are to show the opinions of several learned men, who have carefully considered and wrote expressly on the subject; such as Milton, Locke, Rollin, Turnbull, and others. They generally complain, that the old method is in many respects wrong; but long settled forms are not easily changed. For us, who are now to make a beginning, 'tis, at least, as easy to set out right as wrong; and therefore their sentiments are on this occasion well worth our consideration.

Mr. Rollin says (*Belles Lettres,* p. 249, speaking of the manner of educating youth) "Though it be generally a very wise and judicious rule to avoid all singularity, and to follow the received customs, yet I question whether, in the point we now treat of, this principle does not admit of some exception, and whether we ought not to apprehend the dangers and inconveniencies of blindly following the footsteps of those who have

FRANKLIN'S EDUCATIONAL VIEWS

Many of the first settlers of these provinces, were men who had received a good education in Europe, and to their wisdom and good management we owe much of our present prosperity. But their hands were full, and they could not do all things. The present race are not thought to be generally of equal ability: for though the American youth are allowed not to want capacity; yet the best capacities require cultivation, it being truly with them, as with the best ground, which unless well tilled and sowed with profitable seed, produces only ranker weeds.

That we may obtain the advantages arising from an increase of knowledge, and prevent as much as may be the mischievous consequences that would attend a general ignorance among us, the following hints are offered towards forming a plan for the education of the youth of Pennsylvania, viz.

It is proposed,

THAT some persons of leisure and public spirit, apply

gone before us, so as to consult custom more than reason, and the governing our actions rather by what others do, than by what they should do; from whence it often happens, that an error once established is handed down from age to age, and becomes almost a certain law, from a notion, that we ought to act like the rest of mankind, and follow the example of the greatest number. But human nature is not so happy as to have the greatest number always make the best choice, and we too frequently observe the contrary."

FRANKLIN AND THE ACADEMY

for a charter, by which they may be incorporated, with power to erect an Academy for the education of youth, to govern the same, provide masters, make rules, receive donations, purchase lands, etc. and to add to their number, from time to time such other persons as they shall judge suitable.

That the members of the corporation make it their pleasure, and in some degree their business, to visit the Academy often, encourage and [10] countenance the youth, countenance and assist the masters, and by all means in their power advance the usefulness and reputation of the design; that they look on the students as in some sort their children, treat them with familiarity and affection, and when they have behaved well, and gone through their studies, and are to enter the world, zealously unite, and make all the interest that can be made to establish them,[11] whether in business, offices,

---

[10] Rollin, Vol. II, p. 371, mentions a French gentleman, Mons. Hersan, who, "at his own expense, built a school for the use of poor children, one of the finest in the kingdom; and left a stipend for the master. That he himself taught them very often, and generally had some of them at his table. He clothed several of them; and distributed rewards among them from time to time, in order to encourage them to study."

[11] Something seems wanting in America to incite and stimulate youth to study. In Europe the encouragements to learning are of themselves much greater than can be given here. Whoever distinguishes himself there, in either of the three learned professions, gains fame, and often wealth and power: A

marriages, or any other thing for their advantage, preferably to all other persons whatsoever even of equal merit.

And if men may, and frequently do, catch such a taste for cultivating flowers, for planting, grafting, inoculating, and the like, as to despise all other amusements for their sake, why may not we expect they should acquire a relish for that more useful culture of young minds. Thompson says,

> *'Tis joy to see the human blossoms blow,*
> *When infant reason grows apace, and calls*
> *For the kind hand of an assiduous care;*
> *Delightful task! to rear the tender thought,*
> *To teach the young idea how to shoot,*
> *To pour the fresh instruction o'er the mind,*
> *To breathe th' enliv'ning spirit, and to fix*
> *The generous purpose in the glowing breast.*

That a house be provided for the Academy, if not in the town, not many miles from it; the situation high and dry, and if it may be, not far from a river, hav-

poor man's son has a chance, if he studies hard, to rise, either in the law or the church, to gainful offices or benefices; to an extraordinary pitch of grandeur; to have a voice in parliament, a seat among the peers; as a statesman or first minister to govern nations, and even to mix his blood with princes.

ing a garden, orchard, meadow, and a field or two.
That the house be furnished with a library (if in the
country, if in the town, the town libraries [12] may serve)

[12] Besides the English library begun and carried on by subscription in Philadelphia, we may expect the benefit of another much more valuable in the learned languages, which has been many years collecting with the greatest care, by a gentleman distinguished for his universal knowledge, no less than for his judgment in books. It contains many hundred volumes of the best authors in the best editions, among which are the Polyglot Bible, and Castel's lexicon on it, in 8 large vols. Aldus's *Septuagint, Apocrypha* and *New Testament,* in Greek, and some other editions of the same; most of the fathers; almost all the Greek authors from Homer himself, in divers editions (and one of them in that of Rome, with Eustathius's *Commentaries,* in 4 vols.) to near the end of the 4th century, with divers later, as Photius, Suidas, divers of the Byzantine historians; all the old mathematicians, as Archimedes, Apollonius, Euclid, Ptolemy's *Geography* and *Almagest,* with Theon's *Commentaries* and Diophantus, in the whole above 100 vols. in Greek folios. All the old Roman classics without exception, and some of them in several editions (as all Tully's works in four editions). All Graevius, Gronovius, Salengre's and Poleni's collections of Roman and Greek antiquities, containing above five hundred distinct discourses in 33 tomes, with some hundreds of late authors in Latin, as Vossius, Lipsius, Grotius, etc. A good collection of mathematical pieces, as Newton in all the three editions, Wallis, Huygens, Tacquet, Dechales, etc. in near 100 vols. in all sizes, with some orientals, French and Italian authors, and many more English, etc. A handsome building above 60 feet in front, is now erected in this city, at the private expense of that gentleman, for the reception of this library, where it is soon to be deposited, and remain for the public use, with a valuable yearly income duly to enlarge it; and I have his permission to mention it as an encouragement to the proposed Acad-

with maps of all countries, globes, some mathematical instruments, an apparatus for experiments in natural philosophy, and for mechanics; prints, of all kinds, prospects, buildings, machines, etc.[13]

That the rector be a man of good understanding, good morals, diligent and patient, learned in the languages and sciences, and a correct pure speaker and writer of the English tongue; to have such tutors under him as shall be necessary.

That the boarding scholars diet[14] together, plainly, temperately, and frugally.

That to keep them in health, and to strengthen and render active their bodies, they be frequently[15] ex-

emy; to which this noble benefaction will doubtless be of the greatest advantage, as not only the students, but even the masters themselves, may very much improve by it.

[13] See Turnbull, p. 415, the description of the furniture of the school called the *Instituto* at Bologna, procured by the care and direction of Count Marsigli, and originally at his private expense.

[14] Perhaps it would be best if none of the scholars were to diet abroad. Milton is of that opinion (*Tractate of Education*) for that much time would else be lost, and many ill habits got.

[15] Milton proposes, that an hour and half before dinner should be allowed for exercise, and recommends among other exercises, the handling of arms, but perhaps this may not be thought necessary here. Turnbull, p. 318, says, "Corporal exercise invigorates the soul as well as the body; let one be kept closely to reading, without allowing him any respite from thinking, or any exercise to his body, and were it possible to preserve long, by such a method, his liking to study and knowl-

ercised in running, leaping, wrestling, and swimming,[16] etc.

That they have peculiar habits to distinguish them

edge, yet we should soon find such an one become no less soft in his mind than in his outward man. Both mind and body would thus become gradually too relaxed, too much unbraced for the fatigues and duties of active life. Such is the union between soul and body, that the same exercises which are conducive, when rightly managed, to consolidate or strengthen the former, are likewise equally necessary and fit to produce courage, firmness, and manly vigor, in the latter. For this, and other reasons, certain hardy exercises were reckoned by the ancients an essential part in the formation of a liberal character; and ought to have their place in schools where youth are taught the languages and sciences." See pp. 318 to 323.

[16] 'Tis supposed that every parent would be glad to have their children skilled in swimming, if it might be learnt in a place chosen for its safety, and under the eye of a careful person. Mr. Locke says, p. 9 in his *Treatise of Education:* " 'Tis that saves many a man's life; and the Romans thought it so necessary, that they ranked it with letters; and it was the common phrase to mark one ill educated, and good for nothing, that he had neither learnt to read or swim: *Nec literas didicit nec natare*. But besides the gaining a skill which may serve him at need, the advantages to health by often bathing in cold water during the heat of the summer, are so many, that I think nothing need be said to encourage it."

'Tis some advantage besides, to be free from the slavish terrors many of those feel who cannot swim, when they are obliged to be on the water even in crossing a ferry.

Mr. Hutchinson, [sic] in his *Dialogues concerning Education,* 2 vols. Octavo, lately published, says, vol. 2, p. 297: "I would have the youth accustomed to such exercises as will harden their constitution, as riding, running, swimming, shooting, and the like."

FRANKLIN'S EDUCATIONAL VIEWS

from other youth, if the academy be in or near the town; for this, among other reasons, that their behaviour may be the better observed.

As to their studies, it would be well if they could be taught everything that is useful, and everything that is ornamental: but art is long, and their time is short. It is therefore proposed that they learn those things that are likely to be most useful and most ornamental. Regard being had to the several professions for which they are intended.

All should be taught to write a fair hand, and swift, as that is useful to all. And with it may be learnt something of drawing,[17] by imitation of prints, and some of the first principles of perspective.

Charlemagne, founder of the German Empire, brought up his sons hardily, and even his daughters were inured to industry. Henry the Great of France, saith Mons. Rhodez, "was not permitted by his grandfather to be brought up with delicacy, who well knew that seldom lodgeth other than a mean and feeble spirit in an effeminate and tender body. He commanded that the boy should be accustomed to run, to leap, to climb the rocks and mountains; that by such means he might be inured to labor, etc. His ordinary food also was of coarse bread, beef, cheese and garlic; his clothing plain and coarse, and often he went barefoot and bareheaded." Walker, of education, p. 17, 18.

[17] Drawing is a kind of universal language, understood by all nations. A man may often express his ideas, even to his own countrymen, more clearly with a lead pencil, or a bit of chalk, than with his tongue. And many can understand a figure, that

Arithmetic,[18] accounts, and some of the first principles of geometry and astronomy.

do not comprehend a description in words, though ever so properly chosen. All boys have an early inclination to this improvement, and begin to make figures of animals, ships, machines, etc. as soon as they can use a pen, but for want of a little instruction at that time generally are discouraged, and quit the pursuit.

Mr. Locke says, p. 234: "When your son can write well and quick, I think it may be convenient not only to continue the exercise of his hand in writing, but also to improve the use of it further in drawing; a thing very useful to a gentleman on several occasions; but especially if he travel; as that which helps a man often to express in a few lines well put together, what a whole sheet of paper in writing would not be able to represent and make intelligible. How many buildings may a man see, how many machines and habits meet with, the ideas whereof would be easily retained, and communicated by a little skill in drawing; which being committed to words, are in danger to be lost, or at best but ill retained in the most exact descriptions? I do not mean that I would have him a perfect painter; to be that to any tolerable degree, will require more time than he can spare from his other improvements of greater moment. But so much insight into perspective and skill in drawing, as will enable him to represent tolerably on paper anything he sees, except faces, may, I think, be got in a little time."

Drawing is no less useful to a mechanic than to a gentleman. Several handicrafts seem to require it; as the carpenter's, shipwright's, engraver's, painter's, carver's, cabinet-maker's, gardener's, and other businesses. By a little skill of this kind, the workman may perfect his own idea of the thing to be done, before he begins to work; and show a draft for the encouragement and satisfaction of his employer.

[18] Mr. Locke is of opinion, p. 269, that a child should be early entered in arithmetic, geography, chronology, history and geometry. "Merchants accounts," he says, "if it is not necessary to

FRANKLIN'S EDUCATIONAL VIEWS

The English language might be taught by grammar [19]; in which some of our best writers, as Tillotson,

help a gentleman to get an estate, yet there is nothing of more use and efficacy to make him preserve the estate he has. 'Tis seldom observed that he who keeps an account of his income and expenses, and thereby has constantly under view the course of his domestic affairs, lets them run to ruin; and I doubt not but that many a man gets behind hand before he is aware, or runs farther on when he is once in, for want of this care, or the skill to do it. I would therefore advise all gentlemen to learn perfectly merchants accounts; and not to think 'tis a skill that belongs not to them, because it has received its name, and has been chiefly practised by men of traffic." p. 316.

Not only the skill, but the habit of keeping accounts, should be acquired by all, as being necessary to all.

[19] Mr. Locke, speaking of grammar, p. 252, says, "That to those the greatest part of whose business in this world is to be done with their tongues, and with their pens, it is convenient, if not necessary, that they should speak properly and correctly, whereby they may let their thoughts into other men's minds the more easily, and with the greater impression. Upon this account it is that any sort of speaking so as will make him be understood is not thought enough for a gentleman. He ought to study grammar, among the other helps of speaking well, but it must be the grammar of his own tongue, of the language he uses, that he may understand his own country speech nicely, and speak it properly, without shocking the ears of those it is addressed to with solecisms and offensive irregularities. And to this purpose grammar is necessary; but it is the grammar only of their own proper tongues, and to those who would take pains in cultivating their language, and perfecting their styles. Whether all gentlemen should not do this, I leave to be considered, since the want of propriety and grammatical exactness is thought very misbecoming one of that rank, and usually draws on one guilty of such faults the imputation of having

FRANKLIN AND THE ACADEMY

Addison, Pope, Algernon Sidney, Cato's *Letters,* etc. should be classics. The styles principally to be cultivated,

had a lower breeding and worse company than suits with his quality. If this be so (as I suppose it is) it will be matter of wonder, why young gentlemen are forced to learn the grammars of foreign and dead languages, and are never once told of the grammar of their own tongues. They do not so much as know there is any such thing, much less is it made their business to be instructed in it. Nor is their own language ever proposed to them as worthy their care and cultivating, though they have daily use of it, and are not seldom, in the future course of their lives, judged of by their handsome or awkward way of expressing themselves in it. Whereas the languages whose grammars they have been so much employed in are such as probably they shall scarce ever speak or write; or if upon occasion this should happen, they should be excused for the mistakes and faults they make in it. Would not a Chinese, who took notice of this way of breeding, be apt to imagine, that all our young gentlemen were designed to be teachers and professors of the dead languages of foreign countries, and not to be men of business in their own." Page 255, the same author adds, that "if grammar ought to be taught at any time, it must be to one that can speak the language already; how else can he be taught the grammar of it? This at least is evident from the practice of the wise and learned nations among the ancients. They made it a part of education to cultivate their own, not foreign tongues. The Greeks counted all other nations barbarous, and had a contempt for their languages. And though the Greek learning grew in credit amongst the Romans towards the end of their commonwealth, yet it was the Roman tongue that was made the study of their youth: their own language they were to make use of, and therefore it was their own language they were instructed and exercised in." And, p. 281, "There can scarce be a greater defect (says he) in a gentleman, than not to express himself well either in writing or speaking. But yet I think I may ask the reader whether he doth not know a

being the clear and the concise. Reading should also be taught, and pronouncing, properly, distinctly, em-

great many who live upon their estates, and so, with the name should have the qualities of gentlemen, who cannot so much as tell a story as they should, much less speak clearly and persuasively in any business. This I think not to be so much their fault as the fault of their education." Thus far Locke.

Mons. Rollin, reckons the neglect of teaching their own tongue a great fault in the French universities. He spends a great part of his first vol. of *Belles Lettres,* on that subject; and lays down some excellent rules or methods of teaching French to Frenchmen grammatically, and making them masters therein, which are very applicable to our language but too long to be inserted here. He practised them on the youth under his care with great success.

Mr. Hutchinson, [*sic*] *Dialogues,* p. 297, says, "To perfect them in the knowledge of their mother tongue, they should learn it in the grammatical way, that they may not only speak it purely but be able both to correct their own idiom, and afterwards enrich the language on the same foundation."

Dr. Turnbull, in his *Observations on a Liberal Education,* says, p. 262, "The Greeks, perhaps, made more early advances in the most useful sciences than any youth have done since, chiefly on this account, that they studied no other language but their own. This no doubt saved them very much time; but they applied themselves carefully to the study of their own language, and were early able to speak and write it in the greatest perfection. The Roman youth, though they learned the Greek, did not neglect their own tongue, but studied it more carefully than we now do Greek and Latin, without giving ourselves any trouble about our own tongue."

Mons. Simon, in an elegant discourse of his among the memoirs of the Academy of Belles Lettres at Paris, speaking of the stress the Romans laid on purity of language and graceful pro-

phatically, not with an even tone, which under-does, nor a theatrical, which over-does nature.

nunciation, adds, "May I here make a reflection on the education we commonly give our children? It is very remote from the precepts I have mentioned. Hath the child arrived to six or seven years of age, he mixes with a herd of ill-bred boys at school, where under the pretext of teaching him Latin no regard is had to his mother tongue. And what happens? What we see every day. A young gentleman of eighteen, who has had this education, cannot read. For to articulate the words and join them together, I do not call reading, unless one can pronounce well, observe all the proper stops, vary the voice, express the sentiments, and read with a delicate intelligence. Nor can he speak a jot better. A proof of this is that he cannot write ten lines without committing gross faults; and because he did not learn his own language well in his early years, he will never know it well. I except a few who being afterwards engaged by their profession, or their natural taste, cultivate their minds by study. And yet even they, if they attempt to write, will find by the labor composition costs them what a loss it is not to have learned their language in the proper season. Education among the Romans was upon a quite different footing. Masters of rhetoric taught them early the principles, the difficulties, the beauties, the subtleties, the depths, the riches of their own language. When they went from these schools they were perfect masters of it, they were never at a loss for proper expressions; and I am much deceived if it was not owing to this that they produced such excellent works with so marvellous facility."

Pliny, in his letter to a lady on choosing a tutor for her son, speaks of it as the most material thing in his education that he should have a good Latin master of rhetoric, and recommends Julius Genitor for his eloquent, open and plain faculty of speaking. He does not advise her to a Greek master of rhetoric,

To form their style they should be put on writing letters [20] to each other, making abstracts of what they

though the Greeks were famous for that science; but to a Latin master, because Latin was the boy's mother tongue. In the above quotation from Mons. Simon, we see what was the office and duty of the master of rhetoric.

[20] This Mr. Locke recommends, *Education,* p. 284, and says, "The writing of letters has so much to do in all the occurrences of human life that no gentleman can avoid showing himself in this kind of writing. Occasions will daily force him to make this use of his pen, which, besides the consequences that, in his affairs, the well or ill managing it often draws after it, always lays him open to a severer examination of his breeding, sense and abilities, than oral discourses, whose transient faults dying for the most part with the sound that gives them life, and so not subject to a strict review, more easily escape observation and censure." He adds,

"Had the methods of education been directed to their right end, one would have thought this so necessary a part could not have been neglected, whilst themes and verses in Latin, of no use at all, were so constantly everywhere pressed, to the racking of children's inventions beyond their strength and hindering their cheerful progress by unnatural difficulties. But custom has so ordained it, and who dares disobey? And would it not be very unreasonable to require of a learned country schoolmaster (who has all the tropes and figures in Farnaby's *Rhetoric* at his fingers' ends) to teach his scholar to express himself handsomely in English, when it appears to be so little his business or thought that the boy's mother (despised, 'tis like, as illiterate for not having read a system of logic or rhetoric) outdoes him in it?

"To speak and write correctly gives a grace and gains a favorable attention to what one has to say; and since 'tis English that an Englishman will have constant use of, that is the language he should chiefly cultivate and wherein most care should be taken to polish and perfect his style. To speak or

read or writing the same things in their own words; telling or writing stories lately read, in their own ex-

write better Latin than English may make a man be talked of, but he will find it more to his purpose to express himself well in his own tongue, that he uses every moment, than to have the vain commendation of others for a very insignificant quality. This I find universally neglected, nor no care taken anywhere to improve young men in their own language that they may thoroughly understand and be masters of it. If any one among us have a facility or purity more than ordinary in his mother tongue it is owing to chance, or his genius, or anything rather than to his education or any care of his teacher. To mind what English his pupil speaks or writes is below the dignity of one bred up among Greek and Latin, though he have but little of them himself. These are the learned languages, fit only for learned men to meddle with and teach. English is the language of the illiterate vulgar. Though the great men among the Romans were daily exercising themselves in their own language, and we find yet upon record the names of orators who taught some of their Emperors Latin, though it were their mother tongue. 'Tis plain the Greeks were yet more nice in theirs. All other speech was barbarous to them but their own, and no foreign language appears to have been studied or valued amongst that learned and acute people, though it be past doubt that they borrowed their learning and philosophy from abroad.

"I am not here speaking against Greek and Latin. I think Latin at least ought to be well understood by every gentleman. But whatever foreign languages a young man meddles with, that which he should critically study and labor to get a facility, clearness and elegancy to express himself in, should be his own; and to this purpose he should daily be exercised in it."

To the same purpose writes a person of eminent learning in a letter to Dr. Turnbull: "Nothing certainly (says he) can be of more service to mankind than a right method of educating the youth, and I should be glad to hear . . . to give an example of the great advantage it would be to the rising age, and to our

pressions. All to be revised and corrected by the tutor who should give his reasons, explain the force and import of words, etc.

To form their pronunciation [21] they may be put on

nation. When our public schools were first established the knowledge of Latin was thought learning; and he that had a tolerable skill in two or three languages, though his mind was not enlightened by any real knowledge, was a profound scholar. But it is not so at present, and people confess that men may have obtained a perfection in these and yet continue deeply ignorant. The Greek education was of another kind [which he describes in several particulars, and adds:] They studied to write their own tongue more accurately than we do Latin and Greek. But where is English taught at present? Who thinks it of use to study correctly that language which he is to use every day in his life, be his station ever so high or ever so insignificant? It is in this the nobility and gentry defend their country, and serve their prince in parliament; in this the lawyers plead, the divines instruct, and all ranks of people write their letters and transact all their affairs; and yet who thinks it worth his learning to write this even accurately, not to say politely? Every one is suffered to form his style by chance; to imitate the first wretched model which falls in his way, before he knows what is faulty or can relish the beauties of a just simplicity. Few think their children qualified for a trade till they have been whipped at a Latin school for five or six years, to learn a little of that which they are obliged to forget; when in those years right education would have improved their minds and taught them to acquire habits of writing their own language easily under right direction; and this would have been useful to them as long as they lived." *Introduction,* p. 3, 4, 5.

Since Mr. Locke's time several good grammars have been wrote and published for the use of schools, as Brightland's, Greenwood's, etc.

[21] By pronunciation is here meant the proper modulation of

making declamations, repeating speeches, delivering orations, etc. The tutor assisting at the rehearsals, teaching, advising, correcting their accent, etc.

But if history [22] be made a constant part of their reading, such as the translations of the Greek and Roman historians and the modern histories of ancient Greece

the voice to suit the subject with due emphasis, action, etc. In delivering a discourse in public, designed to persuade, the manner, perhaps, contributes more to success than either the matter or method. Yet the two latter seem to engross the attention of most preachers and other public speakers, and the former to be almost totally neglected.

[22] As nothing teaches (saith Mr. Locke) so nothing delights more than history. The first of these recommends it to the study of grown men, the latter makes me think it the fittest for a young lad who as soon as he is instructed in chronology and acquainted with the several epochs in use in this part of the world, and can reduce them to the Julian period, should then have some history put into his hand. *Education,* p. 276.

Mons. Rollin complains that the college education in France is defective in teaching history, which he thinks may be made of great advantage to youth. This he demonstrates largely in his *Belles Lettres,* to the satisfaction of all that read the book. He lays down the following rules for studying history, viz. 1. To reduce the study to order and method. 2. To observe what relates to usages and customs. 3. To enquire particularly, and above all things, after the truth. 4. To endeavor to find out the causes of the rise and fall of states, of the gaining or losing of battles, and other events of importance. 5. To study the character of the nations and great men mentioned in history. 6. To be attentive to such instructions as concern moral excellency and the conduct of life. 7. Carefully to note everything that relates to religion. Vol. 3, p. 146.

and Rome, etc., may not almost all kinds of useful knowledge be that way introduced to advantage, and with pleasure to the student? As

Geography, by reading with maps and being required to point out the places where the greatest actions were done, to give their old and new names, with the bounds, situation, extent of the countries concerned, etc.

Chronology, by the help of Helvicus or some other writer of the kind who will enable them to tell when those events happened, what princes were cotemporaries, what states or famous men flourished about that time, etc. The several principal epochs to be first well fixed in their memories.

Ancient customs, religious and civil, being frequently mentioned in history will give occasion for explaining them, in which the prints of medals,[23] basso-relievos, and ancient monuments will greatly assist.

Morality,[24] by descanting and making continual observations on the causes of the rise or fall of any man's character, fortune, power, etc. mentioned in history; the advantages of temperance, order, frugality, industry, perseverance, etc. etc.[25] Indeed the general natural

[23] Plenty of these are to be met with in Montfaucon, and other books of antiquities.

[24] For the importance and necessity of moral instructions to youth see the latter notes.

[25] Dr. Turnbull, *Liberal Education,* p. 371, says, "That the

tendency of reading good history must be to fix in the minds of youth deep impressions of the beauty and usefulness of virtue of all kinds, public spirit, fortitude, etc.

History will show the wonderful effects of oratory in governing, turning and leading great bodies of mankind, armies, cities, nations. When the minds of youth are struck with admiration at this,[26] then is the time to give them the principles of that art, which they will

---

useful lessons which ought to be inculcated upon youth are much better taught and enforced from characters, actions and events, developing the inward springs of human conduct and the different consequences of actions, whether with respect to private or public good, than by abstract philosophical lectures. History points out in examples, as in a glass, all the passions of the human heart and all their various workings in different circumstances, all the virtues and all the vices human nature is capable of, all the snares, all the temptations, all the vicissitudes and incidents of human life; and gives occasion for explaining all the rules of prudence, decency, justice and integrity in private economy, and in short all the laws of natural reason."

[26] "Rules are best understood when examples that confirm them and point out their fitness or necessity naturally lead one, as it were by the hand, to take notice of them. One who is persuaded and moved by a speech, and heartily admires its force and beauty, will with pleasure enter into a critical examination of its excellencies and willingly lay up in his mind the rules of rhetoric such an example of eloquence plainly suggests. But to teach rules abstractly, or without examples, and before the agreeable effects the observance of them tends to produce (which are in reality their reason or foundation) have been felt, is exceedingly preposterous." Turnbull, p. 410.

study with taste and application. Then they may be made acquainted with the best models among the ancients, their beauties being particularly pointed out to them. Modern political oratory being chiefly performed by the pen and press, its advantages over the ancient in some respects are to be shown, as that its effects are more extensive, more lasting, etc.

History will also afford frequent opportunities of showing the necessity of a public religion, from its usefulness to the public; the advantage of a religious character among private persons; the mischiefs of superstition, etc. and the excellency of the Christian religion above all others ancient or modern.[27]

History will also give occasion to expatiate on the advantage of civil orders and constitutions, how men and their properties are protected by joining in societies and establishing government, their industry encouraged and rewarded, arts invented, and life made more comfortable: the advantages of liberty, mischiefs of licentiousness, benefits arising from good laws and a due execution of justice, etc. Thus may the first prin-

"I have seldom or never observed any one to get the skill of speaking handsomely by studying the rules which pretend to teach rhetoric." Locke, p. 279.

[27] See Turnbull on this head, from p. 386 to 390, very much to the purpose but too long to be transcribed here.

ciples of sound politics [28] be fixed in the minds of youth.

On historical occasions questions of right and wrong, justice and injustice, will naturally arise, and may be put to youth, which they may debate in conversation and in writing.[29] When they ardently desire victory for the

---

[28] Thus, as Milton says, *Education,* p. 381, should they be instructed in the beginning, end and reasons of political societies; that they may not, in a dangerous fit of the commonwealth, be such poor, shaken, uncertain reeds, of such a tottering conscience as many of our great counsellors have lately shown themselves, but steadfast pillars of the state.

[29] After this they are to dive into the grounds of law and legal justice, delivered first and with best warrant by Moses, and as far as human prudence can be trusted in those celebrated remains of the ancient Grecian and Roman law-givers, etc. p. 382.

"When he has pretty well digested Tully's *Offices,*" says Mr. Locke, p. 277, "and added to it Puffendorff *de Officio Hominis & Civis,* it may be reasonable to set him upon Grotius, *de Jure Belli & Pacis,* or which perhaps is the better of the two, Puffendorff *de Jure Naturali & Gentium;* wherein he will be instructed in the natural rights of men, and the original and foundations of society and the duties resulting from thence. This general part of civil law and history are studies which a gentleman should not barely touch at but constantly dwell upon, and never have done with. A virtuous and well-behaved young man that is well versed in the general part of the civil law (which concerns not the chicane of private cases but the affairs and intercourse of civilized nations in general, grounded upon principles of reason) understands Latin well, and can write a good hand, one may turn loose into the world with great assurance that he will find employment and esteem everywhere."

FRANKLIN'S EDUCATIONAL VIEWS

sake of the praise attending it they will begin to feel the want and be sensible of the use of logic, or the art of reasoning to discover truth and of arguing to defend it, and convince adversaries. This would be the time to acquaint them with the principles of that art. Grotius, Puffendorff, and some other writers of the same kind, may be used on these occasions to decide their disputes. Public disputes [30] warm the imagination, whet the industry, and strengthen the natural abilities.

[30] Mr. Walker, in his excellent *Treatise of the Education of Young Gentlemen,* speaking of public and open argumentation pro and con, says, p. 124, 125: "This is it which brings a question to a point, and discovers the very center and knot of the difficulty. This warms and activates the spirit in the search of truth, excites notions, and by replying and frequent beating upon it cleanseth it from the ashes and makes it shine and flame out the clearer. Besides, it puts them upon a continual stretch of their wits to defend their cause, it makes them quick in replies, intentive upon their subject where the opponent useth all means to drive his adversary from his hold and the answerer defends himself sometimes with the force of truth, sometimes with the subtility of his wit, and sometimes also he escapes in a mist of words and the doubles of a distinction, whilst he seeks all holes and recesses to shelter his persecuted opinion and reputation. This properly belongeth to the disputations which are exercises of young students, who are by these velitations and in this palaestra brought up to a more serious search of truth. And in them I think it not a fault to dispute for victory and to endeavor to save their reputation, nor that their questions and subjects are concerning things of small moment and little reality; yea, I have known some governors that have absolutely forbidden such questions, where the truth was of concernment,

FRANKLIN AND THE ACADEMY

When youth are told that the great men whose lives and actions they read in history spoke two of the best languages that ever were, the most expressive, copious, beautiful; and that the finest writings, the most correct compositions, the most perfect productions of human wit and wisdom, are in those languages, which have endured ages and will endure while there are men; that no translation can do them justice or give the pleasure found in reading the originals; that those languages contain all science; that one of them is become almost universal, being the language of learned men in all countries; that to understand them is a distinguishing ornament, etc. they may be thereby made desirous of learning those languages, and their industry sharpened in the acquisition of them. All intended for divinity should be taught the Latin and Greek; for physic, the Latin, Greek and French; for law, the Latin and French; merchants, the French, German and Spanish; and though all should not be compelled to learn Latin, Greek, or the modern foreign languages, yet none that have an ardent desire to learn them should be refused; their English, arithmetic, and other studies absolutely necessary being at the same time not neglected.

on purpose that the youth might have the liberty of exerting their parts to the uttermost and that there might be not stint to their emulation."

If the new *Universal History* were also read it would give a connected idea of human affairs, so far as it goes, which should be followed by the best modern histories, particularly of our mother country; then of these colonies; which should be accompanied with observations on their rise, increase, use to Great Britain, encouragements, discouragements, etc. the means to make them flourish, secure their liberties, etc.

With the history of men, times and nations should be read, at proper hours or days, some of the best histories of nature,[31] which would not only be delightful

---

[31] Rollin, Vol. 4, p. 211, speaking of natural philosophy, says, "That much of it falls within the capacity of all sorts of persons, even of children. It consists in attending to the objects which nature presents us, in considering them with care, and admiring their different beauties, etc. Searching out their secret causes indeed more properly belongs to the learned.

"I say that even children are capable of studying nature, for they have eyes and don't want curiosity; they ask questions and love to be informed; and here we need only awaken and keep up in them the desire of learning and knowing, which is natural to all mankind. Besides this study, if it is to be called a study, instead of being painful and tedious, is pleasant and agreeable; it may be used as a recreation, and should usually be made a diversion. It is inconceivable how many things children are capable of if all the opportunities of instructing them were laid hold of, with which they themselves supply us.

"A garden, a country, a plantation are all so many books which lie open to them; but they must have been taught and accustomed to read in them. Nothing is more common amongst us than the use of bread and linen. How seldom do children

FRANKLIN AND THE ACADEMY

to youth and furnish them with matter for their letters, etc. as well as other history, but afterwards of great use to them, whether they are merchants, handicrafts, or divines, enabling the first the better to understand many commodities, drugs, etc. the second to improve his

know how either of them are prepared, through how many operations and hands the corn and flax must pass, before they are turned into bread and linen? The same may be said of cloth, which bears no resemblance to the wool whereof it is formed any more than paper to the rags which are picked up in the streets; and why should not children be instructed in these wonderful works of nature and art which they every day make use of without reflecting upon them?

He adds, that a careful master may in this way enrich the mind of his disciple with a great number of useful and agreeable ideas, and by a proper mixture of short reflections will at the same time take care to form his heart and lead him by nature to religion.

Milton also recommends the study of natural philosophy to youth, *Education,* p. 380. "In this," says he, "they may proceed leisurely from the history of meteors, minerals, plants and living creatures as far as anatomy; then also in course might be read to them out of some not tedious writer, the institution of physics; that they may know the tempers, the humours, the seasons, and how to manage a crudity; which he who can wisely and timely do is not only a great physician to himself, and to his friends, but also may at some time or other save an army by this frugal and expenseless means only; and not let the healthy and stout bodies of young men rot away under him for want of this discipline, which is a great pity and no less a shame to the commander."

Proper books may be Ray's *Wisdom of God in the Creation,* Derham's *Physico-Theology, Spectacle de la Nature,* etc.

FRANKLIN'S EDUCATIONAL VIEWS

trade or handicraft by new mixtures, materials, etc. and the last to adorn his discourses by beautiful comparisons and strengthen them by new proofs of Divine Providence. The conversation of all will be improved by it, as occasions frequently occur of making natural observations, which are instructive, agreeable, and entertaining in almost all companies. Natural history will also afford opportunities of introducing many observations relating to the preservation of health, which may be afterwards of great use. Arbuthnot on air and aliment, Sanctorius on perspiration, Lemery on foods, and some others, may now be read, and a very little explanation will make them sufficiently intelligible to youth.

While they are reading natural history might not a little gardening, planting, grafting, inoculating, etc. be taught and practised; and now and then excursions made to the neighboring plantations of the best farmers, their methods observed and reasoned upon for the information of youth. The improvement of agriculture being useful to all,[32] and skill in it no disparagement to any.

---

[32] Milton would have the Latin authors on agriculture taught at school, as Cato, Varro and Columella; "for the matter," says he, "is most easy, and if the language be difficult, yet it may be mastered. And here will be an occasion of inciting and enabling them hereafter to improve the tillage of their country, to

FRANKLIN AND THE ACADEMY

The history of commerce, of the invention of arts, rise of manufactures, progress of trade, change of its seats, with the reasons, causes, etc. may also be made entertaining to youth, and will be useful to all. And this, with the accounts in other history of the prodigious force and effect of engines and machines used in war, will naturally introduce a desire to be instructed in mechanics,[33] and to be informed of the principles of that art by which weak men perform such wonders, labor is saved, manufactures expedited, etc. etc. This will be the time to show them prints of ancient and modern

---

recover the bad soil and to remedy the waste that is made of good; for this was one of Hercules' praises." *Education,* p. 379.

Hutcheson (*Dialogues on Education,* 303, 2nd vol.) says, "Nor should I think it below the dignity or regard of an university to descend even to the general precepts of agriculture and gardening. Virgil, Varro, and others eminent in learning, thought it not below their pen . . . and why should we think meanly of that art which was the mother of heroes and of the masters of the world."

Locke also recommends the study of husbandry and gardening, as well as gaining an insight in several of the manual arts; *Education,* p. 309, 314, 315. It would be a pleasure and diversion to boys to be led now and then to the shops of artificers and suffered to spend some time there in observing their manner of working. For the usefulness of mechanic skill, even to gentlemen, see the pages above cited, to which much might be added.

[33] How many mills are built and machines constructed, at great and fruitless expense, which a little knowledge in the principles of mechanics would have prevented?

machines, to explain them, to let them be copied,[34] and to give lectures in mechanical philosophy.

With the whole should be constantly inculcated and cultivated that benignity of mind,[35] which shows itself in searching for and seizing every opportunity to serve and to oblige; and is the foundation of what is called good breeding; highly useful to the possessor, and most agreeable to all.[36]

---

[34] We are often told in the journals of travellers that such and such things are done in foreign countries, by which labor is saved and manufactures expedited, etc., but their description of the machines or instruments used are quite unintelligible for want of good drafts. Copying prints of machines is of use to fix the attention on the several parts, their proportions, reasons, effects, etc. A man that has been used to this practice is not only better able to make a draft when the machine is before him, but takes so much better notice of its appearance that he can carry it off by memory when he has not the opportunity of drawing it on the spot. Thus may a traveller bring home things of great use to his country.

[35] "Upon this excellent disposition (says Turnbull, p. 326) it will be easy to build that amiable quality commonly called good breeding, and upon no other foundation can it be raised. For whence else can it spring but from a general good-will and regard for all people, deeply rooted in the heart, which makes any one that has it careful not to show in his carriage, any contempt, disrespect, or neglect of them, but to express a value and respect for them according to their rank and condition, suitable to the fashion and way of their country? 'Tis a disposition to make all we converse with easy and well pleased."

[36] "It is this lovely quality which gives true beauty to all other accomplishments, or renders them useful to their possessor, in procuring him the esteem and good-will of all that he comes

FRANKLIN AND THE ACADEMY

The idea of what is true merit should also be often presented to youth, explained and impressed on their minds, as consisting in an inclination joined with an ability to serve mankind, one's country, friends and family; which ability is (with the blessing of God) to be acquired or greatly increased by true learning; and should indeed be the great aim and end [37] of all learning.

---

near. Without it, his other qualities, however good in themselves, make him but pass for proud, conceited, vain or foolish. Courage, says an excellent writer, in an ill-bred man has the air, and escapes not the opinion of brutality; learning becomes pedantry; wit, buffoonery; plainness, rusticity; and there cannot be a good quality in him which ill-breeding will not warp and disfigure to his disadvantage." Turnbull, p. 327.

[37] To have in view the glory and service of God, as some express themselves, is only the same thing in other words. For doing good to men is the only service of God in our power; and to imitate His beneficence is to glorify Him. Hence Milton says, "The end of learning is to repair the ruins of our first parents, by regaining to know God aright, and out of that knowledge to love him, to imitate him, to be like him, as we may the nearest by possessing our souls of true virtue." *Education,* p. 373. Mr. Hutcheson says, *Dialogues,* Vol. 2, p. 97, "The principal end of education is to form us wise and good creatures, useful to others, and happy ourselves. The whole art of education lies within a narrow compass, and is reducible to a very simple practice; namely, to assist in unfolding those natural and moral powers with which man is endowed, by presenting proper objects and occasions; to watch their growth that they be not diverted from their end, or disturbed in their operation by any foreign violence; and gently to conduct and apply them

to all the purposes of private and of public life." And Mr. Locke (p. 84, *Education*) says, " 'Tis virtue, then, direct virtue, which is to be aimed at in education. All other considerations and accomplishments are nothing in comparison to this. This is the solid and substantial good, which tutors should not only read lectures and talk of, but the labor and art of education should furnish the mind with, and fasten there, and never cease till the young man had a true relish of it, and placed his strength, his glory, and his pleasure in it." And Mons. Rollin, *Belles Lettres,* Vol. 4, p. 249, to the same purpose, "If we consult our reason ever so little, it is easy to discern that the end which masters should have in view is not barely to teach their scholars Greek and Latin, to learn them to make exercises and verses, to charge their memory with facts and historical dates, to draw up syllogisms in form, or to trace lines and figures upon paper. These branches of learning I own are useful and valuable, but as means, and not as the end; when they conduct us to other things, and not when we stop at them; when they serve us as preparatives and instruments for better knowledge, without which the rest would be useless. Youth would have cause to complain if they were condemned to spend eight or ten of the best years of their life in learning, at a great expense, and with incredible pains, one or two languages, and some other matters of a like nature, which perhaps they would seldom have occasion to use. The end of masters, in the long course of their studies, is to habituate their scholars to serious application of mind, to make them love and value the sciences, and to cultivate in them such a taste as shall make them thirst after them when they are gone from school; to point out the method of attaining them; and make them thoroughly sensible of their use and value; and by that means dispose them for the different employments to which it shall please God to call them. Besides this, the end of masters should be to improve their hearts and understandings, to protect their innocence, to inspire them with principles of honor and probity, to train them up to good habits; to correct and subdue in them by gentle means the ill inclinations they shall be observed to have, such as pride, insolence,

FRANKLIN AND THE ACADEMY

an high opinion of themselves, and a saucy vanity continually employed in lessening others; a blind self-love solely attentive to its own advantage; a spirit of raillery which is pleased with offending and insulting others; an indolence and sloth, which renders all the good qualities of the mind useless."

Dr. Turnbull has the same sentiments, with which we shall conclude this note. "If," says he, "there be any such thing as duty, or any such thing as happiness, if there be any difference between right and wrong conduct; any distinction between virtue and vice, or wisdom and folly; in fine, if there be any such thing as perfection or imperfection belonging to the rational powers which constitute moral agents; or if enjoyments and pursuits admit of comparison; good education must of necessity be acknowledged to mean proper care to instruct early in the science of happiness and duty, or in the art of judging and acting aright in life. Whatever else one may have learned, if he comes into the world from his schooling and masters, quite unacquainted with the nature, rank and condition of mankind, and the duties of human life (in its more ordinary circumstances at least) he hath lost his time; he is not educated; he is not prepared for the world; he is not qualified for society; he is not fitted for discharging the proper business of man. The way therefore to judge whether education be on a right footing or not is to compare it with the end; or to consider what it does in order to accomplish youth for choosing and behaving well in the various conditions, relations and incidents of life. If education be calculated and adapted to furnish young minds betimes with proper knowledge for their guidance and direction in the chief affairs of the world and in the principal vicissitudes to which human concerns are subject, then is it indeed proper or right education. But if such instruction be not the principal scope to which all other lessons are rendered subservient in what is called the institution of youth, either the art of living and acting well is not man's most important business, or what ought to be the chief end of education is neglected and sacrificed to something of far inferior moment." *Observations on Liberal Education*, p. 175, 176.

FRANKLIN'S EDUCATIONAL VIEWS

II

Constitutions of the Public Academy in the City of Philadelphia [38]

As nothing can more effectually contribute to the cultivation and improvement of a country, the wisdom, riches and strength, virtue and piety, the welfare and happiness of a people, than a proper education of youth by forming their manners, imbuing their tender minds with principles of rectitude and morality, instructing them in the dead and living languages, particularly their mother tongue, and all useful branches of liberal arts and sciences; for attaining these great and important advantages, so far as the present state of our infant country will admit, and laying a foundation for posterity to erect a seminary of learning more extensive and suitable to their future circumstances; an Academy for teaching the Latin and Greek languages, the English tongue grammatically, and as a language, the most useful living foreign languages, French, German and Spanish; as matters of erudition naturally flowing from the languages, history, geography, chronology, logic

---

[38] "The subscribers . . . appointed Mr. Francis, then attorney-general, and myself to draw up constitutions for the government of the Academy. . . ." *Autobiography*. Reprinted from William Kent Gilbert's *History of the College & Academy of Philadelphia* . . . Philadelphia, 1863.

and rhetoric, writing, arithmetic; the several branches of the mathematics; natural and mechanic philosophy; drawing in perspective, and every other part of useful learning and knowledge shall be set up, maintained and have continuance within the city of Philadelphia, in manner following. Twenty-four persons, to wit, James Logan, Thomas Lawrence, William Allen, John Inglis, Tench Francis, William Masters, Lloyd Zachary, Samuel M'Call, Junior, Joseph Turner, Benjamin Franklin, Thomas Leech, William Shippen, Robert Strettell, Philip Syng, Charles Willing, Phineas Bond, Richard Peters, Abraham Taylor, Thomas Bond, Thomas Hopkinson, William Plumstead, Joshua Maddox, Thomas White, and William Coleman, of the city of Philadelphia, shall be Trustees to begin and carry into execution this good and pious undertaking, who shall not for any services by them as Trustees performed claim or receive any reward or compensation; which number shall always be continued, but never exceeded, upon any motive whatever.

When any Trustee shall remove his habitation far from the city of Philadelphia, reside beyond sea, or die, the remaining Trustees shall with all convenient speed proceed to elect another, residing in or near the city, to fill the place of the absenting or deceased person.

The Trustees shall have general conventions once in every month and may, on special occasions, meet at other times on notice, at some convenient place within the city of Philadelphia, to transact the business incumbent on them; and shall, in the *Gazette,* advertise the time and place of their general conventions.

Nothing shall be transacted by the Trustees, or under their authority, alone, unless the same be voted by a majority of their whole number, if at a general convention; and if at a special meeting, by a like majority, upon personal notice given to each Trustee, at least one day before, to attend.

The Trustees shall at their first meeting elect a President for one year, whose particular duty it shall be, when present, to regulate their debates and state the proper questions arising from them, and to order notices to be given of the times and places of their special conventions. And the like election shall be annually made, at their first meeting, after the expiration of each year.

The Trustees shall annually choose one of their own members for a Treasurer, who shall receive all donations and money due to them, and disburse and lay out the same, according to their orders; and at the end of each year pay the sum remaining in his hands to his successor.

All contracts and assurances for payment of money

FRANKLIN AND THE ACADEMY

to them shall be made in the name of the Treasurer for the time being, and declared to be in trust for the use of the Trustees.

The Trustees may appoint a Clerk whose duty in particular it shall be to attend them in their general and special conventions, to give notice in writing to the members of the time, place and design of any special meetings; to register all their proceedings, and extract a state of their accounts annually, to be published in the *Gazette;* for which they may pay him such salary as they shall think reasonable.

The Trustees shall, with all convenient speed, after signing these constitutions, contract with any person that offers, who they shall judge most capable of teaching the Latin and Greek languages, history, geography, chronology and rhetoric; having great regard at the same time to his polite speaking, writing, and understanding the English tongue; which person shall in fact be, and shall be styled, the Rector of the Academy.

The Trustees may contract with the Rector for the term of five years, or less, at their discretion, for the sum of two hundred pounds a year.

The Rector shall be obliged, without the assistance of any usher, to teach twenty scholars the Latin and Greek languages; and at the same time, according to the best of his capacity, to instruct them in history, geography, chronology, logic, rhetoric, and the English tongue; and twenty-five scholars more for every usher provided for him, who shall be entirely subject to his direction.

The Rector shall upon all occasions, consistent with his duty in the Latin school, assist the English master in improving the youth under his care, and superintend the instruction of all the scholars in the other branches of learning taught within the academy, and see that the masters in each art and science perform their duties.

The Trustees shall, with all convenient speed, contract with any person that offers, who they shall judge most capable of teaching the English tongue grammatically and as a language, history, geography, chronology, logic and oratory; which person shall be styled the English master.

The Trustees may contract with the English master for the term of five years, or less, at their discretion, for the sum of one hundred pounds a year.

The English master shall be obliged, without the assistance of any usher, to teach forty scholars the English tongue grammatically and as a language; and at the same time, according to the best of his capacity, to instruct them in history, geography, chronology, logic, and oratory; and sixty scholars more for every usher provided for him.

The ushers for the Latin and Greek school shall be admitted, and at pleasure removed, by the Trustees and the Rector, or a majority of them.

The ushers for the English school shall be admitted, and at pleasure removed, by the Trustees and the English master, or a majority of them.

The Trustees shall contract with each usher to pay him what they shall judge proportionable to his capacity and merit.

Neither the Rector nor English master shall be removed unless disabled by sickness or other natural infirmity, or for gross voluntary neglect of duty, continued after two admonitions from the Trustees, or for committing infamous crimes; and such removal be voted by three-fourths of the trustees, after which their salaries respectively shall cease.

The Trustees shall, with all convenient speed, endeavor to engage persons capable of teaching the French, Spanish, and German languages, writing, arithmetic, the several branches of the mathematics, natural and mechanic philosophy, and drawing; who shall give their attendance as soon as a sufficient number of scholars shall offer to be instructed in those parts of learning, and be paid such salaries and reward as the Trustees shall from time to time be able to allow.

FRANKLIN'S EDUCATIONAL VIEWS

Each scholar shall pay such sum or sums, quarterly, according to the particular branches of learning they shall desire to be taught, as the Trustees shall from time to time settle and appoint.

In case of the disability of the Rector, or any master established on the foundation by receiving a certain salary, through sickness or any other natural infirmity whereby he may be reduced to poverty, the Trustees shall have power to contribute to his support, in proportion to his distress and merit, and the stock in their hands.

For the security of the Trustees, in contracting with the Rector, masters and ushers, to enable them to provide and fit up convenient schools; furnish them with books of general use, that may be too expensive for each scholar; maps, draughts, and other things generally necessary for the improvement of the youth; and to bear the incumbent charges that will unavoidably attend this undertaking, especially in the beginning; the donations of all persons inclined to encourage it are to be cheerfully and thankfully accepted.

The Academy shall be opened with all convenient speed by accepting the first good master that offers, either for teaching the Latin and Greek, or English, under the terms above proposed.

All rules for the attendance and duty of the masters,

the conduct of the youth, and the facilitating their progress in learning and virtue, shall be framed by the masters in conjunction with the Trustees.

If the scholars shall hereafter grow very numerous, and the funds be sufficient, the Trustees may at their discretion augment the salaries of the Rector or master.

The Trustees, to increase their stock, may let their money out at interest.

In general, the Trustees shall have power to dispose of all money received by them as they shall think best for the advantage, promotion, and even the enlargement of this design.

The Trustees may hereafter add to or change any of these constitutions, except that hereby declared to be invariable.

All Trustees, Rectors, masters, ushers, clerks and other ministers, hereafter to be elected or appointed for carrying this undertaking into execution, shall, before they be admitted to the exercise of their respective trusts or duties, sign these constitutions, or some others to be hereafter framed by the Trustees in their stead, in testimony of their then approving of, and resolving to observe them.

Upon the death or absence as aforesaid of any Trustee, the remaining Trustees shall not have authority to exercise any of the powers reposed in them until they

FRANKLIN'S EDUCATIONAL VIEWS

have chosen a new Trustee in his place, and such new Trustee shall have signed the established constitutions; which if he shall refuse to do, they shall proceed to elect another, and so *toties quoties,* until the person elected shall sign the constitutions.

When the fund is sufficient to bear the charge, which it is hoped through the bounty and charity of well disposed persons will soon come to pass, poor children shall be admitted, and taught gratis what shall be thought suitable to their capacities and circumstances.

It is hoped and expected that the Trustees will make it their pleasure, and in some degree their business, to visit the Academy often, to encourage and countenance the youth, countenance and assist the masters, and by all means in their power advance the usefulness and reputation of the design; that they will look on the students as in some measure their own children, treat them with familiarity and affection; and when they have behaved well, gone through their studies, and are to enter the world, they shall zealously unite and make all the interest that can be made to promote and establish them whether in business, offices, marriages, or any other thing for their advantage, preferable to all other persons whatsoever, even of equal merit.

The Trustees shall in a body visit the Academy once a year extraordinary, to view and hear the performances

FRANKLIN AND THE ACADEMY

and lectures of the scholars, in such modes as their respective masters shall think proper; and shall have power, out of their stock, to make presents to the most meritorious scholars, according to their several deserts.

III

Franklin's original interest, as has been noted, was in the creation of facilities for an English education. His *Idea of the English School* was a clear-cut plan for an institution that should prepare for the everyday walks of life. The English school was to have neither ancient nor modern foreign languages. But this purely vernacular institution was given up, owing to the influence of friends, whose judgment and support Franklin valued, in favor of one, the Academy, which was to contain both Latin and English schools. The "Constitutions," given above, show that quite definite provisions were made for classical and vernacular education. Though at first flourishing, the English school began to decline, apparently because of partiality on the part of the Trustees for the Latin school, and its complete abolition was frequently considered. In the "Observations," Franklin reviewed the history of both departments, as shown by the Trustees' records, pointing out that faith had not been kept with the subscribers, and calling for "a separation" from the Latinists so that it might be possible to "execute the plan they have so long defeated, and afford the public the means of a complete English education." The "Observations" are significant in that they show how difficult a matter it was to promote the new, and generally unpopular, realistic education, against the generally conservative opinion of that day, that no education was quite so worthy, dignified, or proper as that gained from the mastery of ancient tongues.

Observations Relative to the Intentions of the Original Founders of the Academy in Philadelphia [39]

As the English school in the Academy has been, and still continues to be, a subject of dispute and discussion among the Trustees since the restitution of the charter,

[39] Sparks, Jared, *The Works of Benjamin Franklin,* Vol II, pp. 133–159, Boston, 1836–1840. This manuscript was given by Franklin to Robert Hare in the summer of 1789, when changes in the system of education in the English school of the College were being considered. It was his intention that it should be submitted to the Trustees, as a testimony of his sentiments, ill health not permitting him to meet with them personally.

FRANKLIN AND THE ACADEMY

and it has been proposed that we should have some regard to the original intention of the founders in establishing that school, I beg leave, for your information, to lay before you what I know of that matter originally, and what I find on the minutes relating to it, by which it will appear how far the design of that school has been adhered to or neglected.

Having acquired some little reputation among my fellow citizens, by projecting the public library in 1732, and obtaining the subscriptions by which it was established; and by proposing and promoting, with success, sundry other schemes of utility in 1749; I was encouraged to hazard another project, that of a public education for our youth. As in the scheme of the library I had provided only for English books, so in this new scheme my ideas went no further than to procure the means of a good English education. A number of my friends, to whom I communicated the proposal, concurred with me in these ideas; but Mr. Allen, Mr. Francis, Mr. Peters, and some other persons of wealth and learning, whose subscriptions and countenance we should need, being of opinion that it ought to include the learned languages, I submitted my judgment to theirs, retaining however a strong prepossession in favor of my first plan, and resolving to preserve as much of it as I could, and to nourish the English school by every means in my power.

FRANKLIN'S EDUCATIONAL VIEWS

Before I went about to procure subscriptions, I thought it proper to prepare the minds of the people by a pamphlet, which I wrote, and printed, and distributed with my newspapers gratis. The title was, *Proposals Relating to the Education of Youth in Pennsylvania.* I happen to have preserved one of them; and, by reading a few passages, it will appear how much the English learning was insisted upon in it; and I had good reasons to know that this was a prevailing part of the motives for subscribing with most of the original benefactors.[40]

---

[40] That the Rector be a man of good understanding, good morals, diligent and patient, learned in the languages and sciences, and a correct, pure speaker and writer of the English tongue; to have such tutors under him as shall be necessary.

The English language might be taught by grammar; in which some of our best writers, as Tillotson, Addison, Pope, Algernon Sidney, Cato's *Letters,* etc. should be classics; the styles principally to be cultivated being the clear and the concise. Reading should also be taught, and pronouncing properly, distinctly, emphatically; not with an even tone, which under-does, nor a theatrical, which over-does nature.

Mr. Locke, speaking of grammar, (p. 252,) says, that "To those, the greatest part of whose business in this world is to be done with their tongue, and with their pens, it is convenient, if not necessary, that they should speak properly and correctly, whereby they may let their thoughts into other men's minds the more easily, and with the greater impression. Upon this account it is, that any sort of speaking, so as will make him be understood, is not thought enough for a gentleman. He ought to study grammar, among the other helps of speaking well; but it must be the grammar of his own tongue, of the lan-

FRANKLIN AND THE ACADEMY

I met with but few refusals in soliciting the subscriptions; and the sum was the more considerable, as I had put the contribution on this footing, that it was not to be immediate, and the whole paid at once, but in parts, a fifth annually during five years. To put the machine

guage he uses, that he may understand his own country speech nicely, and speak it properly, without shocking the ears of those it is addressed to with solecisms and offensive irregularities. And to this purpose grammar is necessary; but it is the grammar only of their own proper tongues, and to those who would take pains in cultivating their language and perfecting their styles. Whether all gentlemen should not do this, I leave to be considered; since the want of propriety and grammatical exactness is thought very misbecoming one of that rank, and usually draws on one, guilty of such faults, the imputation of having had a lower breeding and worse company than suit with his quality. If this be so, (as I suppose it is,) it will be matter of wonder, why young gentlemen are forced to learn the grammars of foreign and dead languages, and are never once told of the grammar of their own tongues. They do not so much as know there is any such thing, much less is it made their business to be instructed in it. Nor is their own language ever proposed to them as worthy their care and cultivating, though they have daily use of it, and are not seldom in the future course of their lives judged of by their handsome or awkward way of expressing themselves in it. Whereas the languages, whose grammars they have been so much employed in, are such as probably they shall scarce ever speak or write; or, if upon occasion this should happen, they should be excused for the mistakes and faults they make in it. Would not a Chinese, who took notice of this way of breeding, be apt to imagine that all our young gentlemen were designed to be teachers and professors of the dead languages of foreign countries, and not to be men of business in their own?

in motion, twenty-four of the principal subscribers agreed to take upon themselves the trust; and a set of constitutions for their government, and for the regulation of the schools, were drawn up by Mr. Francis and myself, which were signed by us all, and printed, that

> The same author adds, (p. 255,) "That if grammar ought to be taught at any time, it must be to one that can speak the language already; how else can he be taught the grammar of it? This at least is evident from the practice of the wise and learned nations among the ancients. They made it a part of education, to cultivate their own, not foreign tongues. The Greeks counted all other nations barbarous, and had a contempt for their languages. And though the Greek learning grew in credit among the Romans towards the end of their commonwealth, yet it was the Roman tongue that was made the study of their youth. Their own language they were to make use of, and therefore it was their own language they were instructed and exercised in." And, (p. 281,) "There can scarce be a greater defect," says he, "in a gentleman, than not to express himself well either in writing or speaking. But yet I think I may ask the reader, whether he doth not know a great many, who live upon their estates, and so, with the name, should have the qualities of gentlemen, who cannot so much as tell a story as they should, much less speak clearly and persuasively in any business. This I think not to be so much their fault as the fault of their education." Thus far Locke.
>
> Monsieur Rollin reckons the neglect of teaching their own tongue a great fault in the French universities. He spends great part of his first volume of *Belles Lettres* on that subject; and lays down some excellent rules or methods of teaching French to Frenchmen grammatically, and making them masters therein, which are very applicable to our language, but too long to be inserted here. He practised them on the youth under his care with great success.

the public might know what was to be expected. I wrote also a paper, entitled, *Idea of an English School,* which was printed, and afterwards annexed to Mr. Peters' Sermon, preached at the opening of the Academy. This paper was said to be for the consideration of the Trustees; and the expectation of the public, that the idea

Mr. Hutchinson, [*sic*] (*Dialogues,* p. 297,) says, "To perfect them in the knowledge of their mother tongue, they should learn it in the grammatical way, that they not only speak it purely, but be able both to correct their own idiom, and afterwards enrich the language on the same foundation."

Dr. Turnbull, in his *Observations on a Liberal Education,* says, (p. 262,) "The Greeks, perhaps, made more early advances in the most useful sciences than any youth have done since, chiefly on this account, that they studied no other language but their own. This, no doubt, saved them very much time; but they applied themselves carefully to the study of their own language, and were early able to speak and write it in the greatest perfection. The Roman youth, though they learned the Greek, did not neglect their own tongue, but studied it more carefully than we now do Greek and Latin, without giving ourselves any trouble about our own tongue."

Monsieur Simon, in an elegant *Discourse* of his among the *Memoirs of the Academy of Belles Lettres* at Paris, speaking of the stress the Romans laid on purity of language and graceful pronunciation, adds, "May I here make a reflection on the education we commonly give our children? It is very remote from the precepts I have mentioned. Hath the child arrived to six or seven years of age, he mixes with a herd of ill-bred boys at school, where, under the pretext of teaching him Latin, no regard is had to his mother tongue. And what happens? What we see every day. A young gentleman of eighteen, who has had this education, cannot read. For to articulate the words, and join them together, I do not call reading, unless one can pro-

might in a great measure be carried into execution, contributed to render the subscriptions more liberal as well as more general. I mention my concern in these transactions, to show the opportunity I had of being well informed in the points I am relating.

nounce well, observe all the proper stops, vary the voice, express the sentiment, and read with a delicate intelligence. Nor can he speak a jot better. A proof of this is, that he cannot write ten lines without committing gross faults; and, because he did not learn his own language well in his early years, he will never know it well. I except a few, who, being afterwards engaged by their profession, or their natural taste, cultivate their minds by study. And yet even they, if they attempt to write, will find by the labor composition costs them, what a loss it is, not to have learned their language in the proper season. Education among the Romans was upon a quite different footing. Masters of rhetoric taught them early the principles, the difficulties, the beauties, the subtleties, the depths, the riches of their own language. When they went from these schools, they were perfect masters of it, they were never at a loss for proper expressions; and I am much deceived if it was not owing to this, that they produced such excellent works with so marvellous facility."

Pliny, in his letter to a lady on choosing a tutor for her son, speaks of it as the most material thing in his education, that he should have a good Latin master of rhetoric, and recommends Julius Genitor for his eloquent, open, and plain faculty of speaking. He does not advise her to a Greek master of rhetoric, though the Greeks were famous for that science; but to a Latin master, because Latin was the boy's mother tongue. In the above quotation from Monsieur Simon, we see what was the office and duty of the master of rhetoric.

To form their style, they should be put on writing letters to each other, making abstracts of what they read; or writing the

FRANKLIN AND THE ACADEMY

These constitutions are upon record in your minutes; and, although the Latin and Greek are by them to be taught, the original idea of a complete English educa-

same things in their own words; telling or writing stories lately read, in their own expressions. All to be revised and corrected by the tutor, who should give his reasons, explain the force and import of words, etc.

This Mr. Locke recommends, (*Education,* p. 284,) and says: "The writing of letters has so much to do in all the occurrences of human life, that no gentleman can avoid showing himself in this kind of writing. Occasions will daily force him to make this use of his pen, which, besides the consequence that, in his affairs, the well or ill managing it often draws after it, always lays him open to a severer examination of his breeding, sense, and abilities, than oral discourses, whose transient faults, dying for the most part with the sound that gives them life, and so not subject to a strict review, more easily escape observation and censure."

He adds: "Had the methods of education been directed to their right end, one would have thought this so necessary a part could not have been neglected, whilst themes and verses in Latin, of no use at all, were so constantly everywhere pressed, to the racking of children's invention beyond their strength, and hindering their cheerful progress by unnatural difficulties. But custom has so ordained it, and who dares disobey? And would it not be very unreasonable to require of a learned country-schoolmaster (who has all the tropes and figures in Farnaby's *Rhetoric* at his fingers' ends) to teach his scholar to express himself handsomely in English, when it appears to be so little his business or thought, that the boy's mother (despised, 'tis like, as illiterate for not having read a system of logic or rhetoric) outdoes him in it?

"To speak and write correctly gives a grace, and gains a favorable attention to what one has to say. And since 'tis English that an Englishman will have constant use of, that is the

FRANKLIN'S EDUCATIONAL VIEWS

tion was not forgotten, as will appear by the following extracts.

Page 1. "The English tongue is to be taught grammatically, and as a language."

language he should chiefly cultivate, and wherein most care should be taken to polish and perfect his style. To speak or write better Latin than English may make a man be talked of; but he will find it more to his purpose to express himself well in his own tongue, that he uses every moment, than to have the vain commendations of others for a very insignificant quality. This I find universally neglected, nor no care taken anywhere to improve young men in their own language, that they may thoroughly understand and be masters of it. If any one among us have a facility or purity more than ordinary in his mother tongue, it is owing to chance, or his genius, or anything, rather than to his education or any care of his teacher. To mind what English his pupil speaks or writes, is below the dignity of one bred up among Greek and Latin, though he have but little of them himself. These are the learned languages, fit only for learned men to meddle with and teach; English is the language of the illiterate vulgar. Though the great men among the Romans were daily exercising themselves in their own language; and we find yet upon the record the names of orators who taught some of their Emperors Latin, though it were their mother tongue. 'Tis plain the Greeks were yet more nice in theirs. All other speech was barbarous to them but their own, and no foreign language appears to have been studied or valued amongst that learned and acute people; though it be past doubt that they borrowed their learning and philosophy from abroad."

To the same purpose writes a person of eminent learning in a letter to Dr. Turnbull. "Nothing, certainly," says he, "can be of more service to mankind than a right method of educating the youth, and I should be glad to hear . . . to give an example of the great advantage it would be to the rising age, and to our nation. When our public schools were first established, the

FRANKLIN AND THE ACADEMY

Page 4. In reciting the qualification of the person to be appointed Rector, it is said, "that *great regard* is to be

knowledge of Latin was thought learning; and he that had a tolerable skill in two or three languages, though his mind was not enlightened by any real knowledge, was a profound scholar. But it is not so at present; and people confess, that men may have obtained a perfection in these, and yet continue deeply ignorant. The Greek education was of another kind," [which he describes in several particulars, and adds:] "They studied to write their own tongue more accurately than we do Latin and Greek. But where is English taught at present? Who thinks it of use to study correctly that language which he is to use every day in his life, be his station ever so high, or ever so insignificant. It is in this the nobility and gentry defend their country, and serve their prince in parliament; in this the lawyers plead, the divines instruct, and all ranks of people write their letters, and transact all their affairs; and yet who thinks it worth his learning to write this even accurately, not to say politely? Every one is suffered to form his style by chance; to imitate the first wretched model which falls in his way, before he knows what is faulty, or can relish the beauties of a just simplicity. Few think their children qualified for a trade till they have been whipped at a Latin school for five or six years, to learn a little of that which they are obliged to forget; when in those years right education would have improved their minds, and taught them to acquire habits of writing their own language easily under right direction; and this would have been useful to them as long as they lived." *Introduction,* pp. 3–5.

To form their pronunciation, they may be put on making declamations, repeating speeches, delivering orations, etc.; the tutor assisting at the rehearsals, teaching, advising, correcting their accent, etc. By pronunciation is here meant, the proper modulation of the voice, to suit the subject with due emphasis, action, etc. In delivering a discourse in public, designed to persuade, the manner, perhaps, contributes more to success, than

had to his *polite speaking, writing, and understanding the English tongue."*

"The Rector was to have two hundred pounds a year, for which he was to be obliged to teach twenty boys, without any assistance (and twenty-five more for every usher provided for him), the Latin and Greek languages; and at the same time instruct them in history, geography, chronology, logic, rhetoric, and *the English tongue."*

"The Rector was also, on all occasions consistent with his duty in the Latin school, to *assist the English master in improving the youth under his care."*

Page 5. "The Trustees shall, with all convenient speed, contract with any person that offers, whom they shall judge most capable of *teaching the English tongue grammatically and as a language,* history, geography, chronology, logic, and oratory; which person shall be styled *the English master."*

The English master was to have one hundred pounds a year, for which he was to teach, without any assistance, forty scholars *the English tongue grammatically;* and at the same time instruct them in history, geography, chronology, logic, and oratory; and sixty scholars more for every usher provided for him.

either the matter or method. Yet the two latter seem to engross the attention of most preachers and other public speakers, and the former to be almost totally neglected.

FRANKLIN AND THE ACADEMY

It is to be observed in this place, that here are two distinct courses in the same study, that is, of the same branches of science, viz. history, geography, chronology, logic, and oratory, to be carried on at the same time, but not by the same tutor or master. The English master is to teach his scholars all those branches of science, and also the English tongue grammatically, as a language. The Latin master is to teach the same sciences to his boys, besides the Greek and Latin. He was also to assist the English master occasionally, without which, and his general care in the government of the schools, the giving him double salary seems not well accounted for. But here are plainly two distinct schools or courses of education provided for. The Latin master was not to teach the English scholars logic, rhetoric, etc.; that was the duty of the English master; but he was to teach those sciences to the Latin scholars. We shall see, hereafter, how easily this original plan was defeated and departed from.

When the constitutions were first drawn, blanks were left for the salaries, and for the number of boys the Latin master was to teach. The first instance of partiality, in favor of the Latin part of the institution, was in giving the title of Rector to the Latin master, and no title to the English one. But the most striking instance was, when we met to sign, and the blanks were first to be filled up, the votes of a majority carried it to give twice as much salary to the Latin master as to the English, and yet require twice as much duty from the English master as from the Latin, viz. £200 to the Latin master to teach twenty boys; £100 to the English master to teach forty! However, the Trustees who voted these salaries being themselves by far the greatest subscribers, though not the most numerous, it was thought they had a kind of right to predominate in money matters; and those, who had wished an equal regard might have been shown to both schools, submitted, though not without regret, and at times some little complaining, which, with their not being able in nine months to find a proper person for *English master,* who would undertake the office for so low a salary, induced the Trustees at length, viz. in July, 1750, to offer £50 more.

Another instance of the partiality above mentioned was in the March preceding, when £100 sterling was voted to buy *Latin* and *Greek* books, maps, drafts, and instruments for the use of the Academy, and nothing for the *English books.*

The great part of the subscribers, who had the English education chiefly in view, were however soothed into a submission to these partialities, chiefly by the expectation given them by the constitution, viz. that the Trustees would make it their pleasure, and in some de-

FRANKLIN AND THE ACADEMY

their colleagues to that school, and obtain acknowledgments of the unjust neglect it had been treated with; of this the following extracts from the minutes are authentic proofs, viz. (Minute Book, Vol. I., February 8th, 1763;) "The state of the English school was taken into consideration, and it was observed, that Mr. Kinnersley's time was entirely taken up in teaching little boys the elements of the English language (this is what it dwindled into, a school similar to those kept by old women, who teach children their letters); and that speaking and rehearsing in public were *totally disused,* to the great prejudice of the other scholars and students, and contrary to the *original design* of the Trustees in the forming of that school; and, as this was a matter of great importance, it was *particularly recommended* to be *fully considered* by the Trustees at their next meeting." At their next meeting it was not considered; but this minute contains full proof of the fact, that the English education had been neglected, and it contains an acknowledgment that the conduct of the English school was contrary to the original design of the Trustees in forming it.

In the same book of minutes we find the following, of April 12th, 1763. "The state of the English school was again taken into consideration; and it was the opinion of the Trustees that the *original design* should be prosecuted, of teaching the scholars (of that and the other schools) the elegance of the English language, and giving them a proper pronunciation; and that the *old method* of hearing them read and repeat in public should be again used. And a committee was appointed to confer with Mr. Kinnersley how this might best be done, as well as what assistance would be necessary to give Mr. Kinnersley to enable him to attend this *necessary service,* which was indeed the *proper business* of his professorship."

In this minute we have another acknowledgment of what was the *original design* of the English school; but here are some words thrown in to countenance an innovation, which had been for some time practised. The words are, "and the other schools." Originally, by the constitutions, the Rector was to teach the Latin scholars their English. The words of the constitution are, "The Rector shall be obliged, without the assistance of any usher, to teach twenty scholars the Latin and Greek languages, and the English tongue." To enable him to do this, we have seen that some of his qualifications, indispensably required, were, his *polite speaking, writing,* and *understanding the English tongue.* Having these, he was enjoined, on all occasions consistent with his other duties, to assist the English master in improving the boys under his care; but there is not a word obliging the English master to teach the Latin boys English. However, the Latin masters, either unable to do it, or unwilling to take the trouble, had got him up among them, and employed so much of his time, that this minute owns he could not, without farther assistance, attend the *necessary service* of his own school, which, as the minute expressly says, "was indeed the *proper business* of his professorship."

Notwithstanding this good resolution of the Trustees, it seems the execution of it was neglected; and, the public not being satisfied, they were again haunted by the friends of the children with the old complaint, that the original constitutions were not complied with, in regard to the English school. Their situation was unpleasant. On the one hand, there were still remaining some of the first Trustees, who were friends to the scheme of English education, and these would now and then be remarking that it was neglected, and would be moving for a reformation; the constitutions at the same time, staring the Trustees in the face, gave weight to these remarks. On the other hand, the Latinists were combined to decry the English school as useless. It was without example, they said, as indeed they still say, that a school for teaching the vulgar tongue, and the sciences in that tongue, was ever joined with a college, and that the Latin masters were fully competent to teach the English.

I will not say that the Latinists looked on every expense upon the English school as so far disabling the Trustees from augmenting their salaries, and therefore regarding it with an evil eye; but, when I find the minutes constantly filled with their applications for higher wages, I cannot but see their great regard for money matters, and suspect a little their using their interest and influence to prevail with the Trustees not to encourage that school. And, indeed, the following minute is so different in spirit and sentiment from that last recited, that one cannot avoid concluding that some extraordinary pains must have been taken with the Trustees between the two meetings of April 12th and June 13th, to produce a resolution so very different, which here follows in this minute, viz. "June 13th, 1763; some of the parents of the children in the Academy having complained that their children were not taught to speak and read in public, and having requested that this useful part of education might be more attended to, Mr. Kinnersley was called in, and desired to give an account of what was done in this branch of his duty; and he declared that this was well taught, not only in the English school, which was more immediately under his care,

FRANKLIN AND THE ACADEMY

but in the philosophy classes, regularly every Monday afternoon, and as often at other times as his other business would permit. And it not appearing to the Trustees that any more could at present be done, without partiality and great inconvenience, and that this was all that was ever proposed to be done, they did not incline to make any alteration, or to lay any farther burden on Mr. Kinnersley." Note here, that the English school had not for some years preceding been visited by the Trustees. If it had, they would have known the state of it without making this inquiry of the master. They might have judged, whether the children more immediately under his care were in truth well taught, without taking his word for it, as it appears they did. But it seems he had a merit, which, when he pleaded it, effectually excused him. He spent his time when out of the English school in instructing the philosophy classes who were of the Latin part of the institution. Therefore they did not think proper to lay any further burden upon him.

It is a little difficult to conceive how these Trustees could bring themselves to declare, that "No more could be done in the English school than was then done, and that it was *all* that *was ever* proposed to be done;" when their preceding minute declares, that "the *original design* was teaching scholars the elegance of the English

FRANKLIN'S EDUCATIONAL VIEWS

language, and giving them a proper pronunciation; and that hearing them read and repeat in public was the *old method,* and should be again used." And certainly, the method that had been used might be again used, if the Trustees had thought fit to order Mr. Kinnersley to attend his own school, and not spend his time in the philosophy classes, where his duty did not require his attendance. What the apprehended partiality was, which the minute mentions, does not appear, and cannot easily be imagined; and the great inconvenience of obliging him to attend his own school could only be depriving the Latinists of his assistance, to which they had no right.

The Trustees may possibly have supposed, that by this resolution they had precluded all future attempts to trouble them with respect to their conduct of the English school. The parents indeed, despairing of any reformation, withdrew their children, and placed them in private schools, of which several now appeared in the city, professing to teach what had been promised to be taught in the Academy; and they have since flourished and increased by the scholars the Academy might have had, if it had performed its engagements. But the public was not satisfied; and we find, five years after, the English school appearing again, after five years' silence, haunting the Trustees like an evil conscience, and reminding them of their failure in duty. For, of their meetings Jan. 19th and 26th, 1768, we find these minutes. "Jan. 19th, 1768; it having been remarked, that the schools suffer in the public esteem by the discontinuance of public speaking, a special meeting is to be called on Tuesday next, to consider the state of the English school and to regulate such matters as may be necessary." "Jan. 26th; a special meeting. It is agreed to give Mr. Jon. Easton and Mr. Thomas Hall, at the rate of twenty-five pounds per annum each, for assisting Mr. Kinnersley in the English school, and taking care of the same when he shall be employed in teaching the students, in the *philosophy classes* and *grammar school,* the art of public speaking. A committee, Mr. Peters, Mr. Coxe, and Mr. Duché, with the masters, was appointed to fix rules and times for employing the youth in public speaking. Mr. Easton and Mr. Hall are to be paid out of a fund to be raised by some public performance for the benefit of the College."

It appears from these minutes, 1. That the reputation of the Academy had suffered in the public esteem by the Trustees' neglect of that school. 2. That Mr. Kinnersley, whose sole business it was to attend it, had been called from his duty and employed in the philosophy classes and Latin grammar school, teaching the scholars there the art of public speaking, which the Latinists used to boast they could teach themselves. 3. That the neglect for so many years of the English scholars, by this subtraction of their master, was now acknowledged, and proposed to be remedied for the future by engaging two persons, Mr. Hall and Mr. Easton, at twenty-five pounds per annum, to take care of those scholars, while Mr. Kinnersley was employed among the Latinists.

Care was however taken by the Trustees, not to be at any expense for this assistance to Mr. Kinnersley; for Hall and Easton were only to be paid out of the uncertain fund of money to be raised by some public performance for the benefit of the College.

A committee was however now appointed to fix rules and times for employing the youth in public speaking. Whether anything was done in consequence of these minutes, does not appear; no report of the committee respecting their doings being to be found on the records, and the probability is that they did, as heretofore, nothing to the purpose. For the English school continued to decline, and the first subsequent mention we find made of it, is in the minute of March 21st, 1769, when the design began to be entertained of abolishing it altogether, whereby the Latinists would get rid of an eyesore, and the Trustees of what occasioned them such frequent trouble. The minute is this; "The state of the

FRANKLIN AND THE ACADEMY

English school is to be taken into consideration at next meeting, and whether it be proper to continue it on its present footing or not." This consideration was, however, not taken at the next meeting, at least nothing was concluded so as to be minuted; nor do we find any farther mention of the English school till the 18th of July, when the following minute was entered; viz. "A special meeting is appointed to be held on Monday next, and notice to be given, that the design of this meeting is to consider whether the English school is to be longer continued."

This special meeting was accordingly held on the 23d of July, 1769, of which date is the following minute and resolution; viz. "The Trustees at this meeting, as well as several former ones, having taken into their serious consideration the state of the English school, are unanimously of opinion, that, as the said school is far from defraying the expense at which they now support it, and not thinking that they ought to lay out any great part of the funds intrusted to them on this branch of education, which can so easily be procured at other schools in this city, have resolved, that, from and after the 17th of October next, Mr. Kinnersley's present salary do cease, and that from that time the said school, if he shall be inclined to keep it, shall be on the following footing; viz. that he shall have the free use of the room where he now teaches, and also the whole tuition-money arising from the boys that may be taught by him, and that he continue professor of English and oratory, and, as such, have the house he lives in rent-free, in consideration of his giving two afternoons in the week as heretofore, for the instruction of the students belonging to the College in public speaking, agreeable to such rules as are or shall be made for that purpose by the Trustees and faculty. It is further ordered by this regulation, that the boys belonging to his school shall be still considered as part of the youth belonging to the College, and under the same general government of the Trustees and faculty; and such of his scholars as may attend the mathematical or any other master having a salary from the College, for any part of their time, shall pay proportionably into the fund of the Trustees, to be accounted for by Mr. Kinnersley, and deducted out of the twenty pounds per quarter now paid by the English scholars."

The Trustees hope this regulation may be agreeable to Mr. Kinnersley, as it proceeds entirely from the reasons set forth above, and not from any abatement of that esteem which they have always retained for him, during the whole course of his services in [the] College.

Upon this and some of the preceding minutes, may be observed; 1. That, the English school having been long neglected, the scholars were so diminished in number as to be far from defraying the expense in supporting it. 2. That, the instruction they received there, instead of a complete English education, which had been promised to the subscribers by the original constitutions, were only such as might easily be procured at other schools in this city. 3. That this unprofitableness of the English school, owing to neglect of duty in the Trustees, was now offered as a reason for demolishing it altogether. For it was easy to see, that, after depriving the master of his salary, he could not long afford to continue it. 4. That if the insufficiency of the tuition-money in the English school to pay the expense, and the ease with which the scholars might obtain equal instruction in other schools, were good reasons for depriving the master of his salary and destroying that school, they were equally good for dismissing the Latin masters, and sending their scholars to other schools; since it is notorious that the tuition-money of the Latin school did not pay much above a fourth part of the salaries of the masters. For such reasons the Trustees might equally well have got rid of all the scholars and all the masters, and remained in full possession of all the College property, without any future expense. 5. That by their refusing any longer to support, instead of reforming, as they ought to have done, the English school, they shamefully broke through and set at nought the original constitutions, for the due execution of which the faith of the original Trustees had been solemnly pledged to the public, and diverted the revenues, proceeding from much of the first subscriptions, to other purposes than those which had been promised. Had the Assembly, when disposed to disfranchise the Trustees, set their foot upon this ground, their proceeding to declare the forfeiture would have been more justifiable; and it may be hoped care will now be taken not to give any future Assembly the same handle.

It seems, however, that this unrighteous resolve did not pass the Trustees without a qualm in some of them. For at the next meeting a reconsideration was moved, and we find the following minute under the date of August 1st, 1769; "The minute of last meeting relative to the English school was read, and after mature deliberation and reconsidering the same, it was voted to stand as it is, provided it should not be found any way repugnant to the first charter granted to the Academy, a copy of which was ordered to be procured out of the rolls office."

One might have thought it natural for the Trustees to have consulted this charter before they took the resolution, and not only the first charter, but the original constitutions; but, as it seems they had lost the instru-

Europe find purchasers for more than 300 copies of any ancient authors. But, printing beginning now to make books cheap, the readers increased so much as to make it worth while to write and print books in the vulgar tongues. At first these were chiefly books of devotion and little histories; gradually several branches of science began to appear in the common languages, and at this day the whole body of science, consisting not only of translations from all the valuable ancients, but of all the new modern discoveries, is to be met with in those languages, so that learning the ancient for the purpose of acquiring knowledge is become absolutely unnecessary.

But there is in mankind an unaccountable prejudice in favor of ancient customs and habitudes, which inclines to a continuance of them after the circumstances, which formerly made them useful, cease to exist. A multitude of instances might be given, but it may suffice to mention one. Hats were once thought an useful part of dress; they kept the head warm and screened it from the violent impression of the sun's rays, and from the rain, snow, hail, etc. Though, by the way, this was not the more ancient opinion or practice; for among all the remains of antiquity, the bustos, statues, basso-relievos, medals, etc., which are infinite, there is no representation of a human figure with a cap or hat on, nor any

FRANKLIN AND THE ACADEMY

ment containing the charter, and, though it had been printed, not one of them was furnished with a copy to which he might refer, it is no wonder that they had forgot the constitutions made twenty years before, to which they do not seem to have in the least adverted.

Probably, however, the Trustees found, when they came to examine original papers, that they could not easily get entirely rid of the English school, and so concluded to continue it. For I find in a law for premiums, minuted under the date of Jan. 29th, 1770, that the English and mathematical school is directed to be examined the third Tuesday in July, and a premium book of the value of one dollar was to be given to him that reads best, and understands best the English grammar, etc. This is very well; but to keep up the old partiality in favor of the Latin school, the premium to its boys was to be of the value of two dollars. In the premiums for best speaking, they were indeed put upon an equality.

After reading this law for premiums, I looked forward to the third Tuesday in July with some pleasing expectation of their effect on the examination required for that day. But I met with only this further record of the inattention of the Trustees to their new resolutions and even laws, when they contained anything favorable to the English school. The minute is only this: "July, August, September, October, no business done."

FRANKLIN'S EDUCATIONAL VIEWS

On the 20th of November, however, I find there was an examination of the Latin school, and premiums, with pompous inscriptions, afterwards adjudged to Latin scholars, but I find no mention of any to the English, or that they were even examined. Perhaps there might have been none to examine, or the school discontinued; for it appears by a minute of July 21st, following, that the provost was desired to advertise for a master able to teach English grammatically, which it seems was all the English master was now required to teach, the other branches originally promised being dropped entirely.

In October, 1772, Mr. Kinnersley resigned his professorship, when Dr. Peters and others were appointed to consider on what footing the English school shall be put for the future, that a new master may be thought of, and Mr. Willing to take care of the school for the present at fifty pounds per annum. It is observable here that there is no mention of putting it on its original footing, and the salary is shrunk amazingly; but this resignation of Mr. Kinnersley gave occasion to one testimony of the utility of the English professor to the institution, notwithstanding all the partiality, neglect, slights, discouragements, and injustice that school had suffered. We find it in the minutes of a special meeting on the 2d of February, 1773, present Dr. Peters, Mr.

FRANKLIN AND THE ACADEMY

Chew, Mr. Lawrence, Mr. Willing, Mr. Trettel, and Mr. Inglis, and expressed in these strong terms.

"The College suffers *greatly* since Mr. Kinnersley left it, for want of a person to teach public speaking, so that the present classes have not those opportunities of learning to declaim and speak which have been of so much *use* to their predecessors, and have contributed *greatly* to *raise the credit* of the institution."

Here is another confession that the Latinists were unequal to the task of teaching English eloquence, though on occasion the contrary is still asserted.

I flatter myself, Gentlemen, that it appears by this time pretty clearly from our own minutes, that the original plan of the English school has been departed from; that the subscribers to it have been disappointed and deceived, and the faith of the Trustees not kept with them; that the public have been frequently dissatisfied with the conduct of the Trustees, and complained of it; that, by the niggardly treatment of good masters, they have been driven out of the school, and the scholars have followed, while a great loss of revenue has been suffered by the Academy; so that the numerous schools now in the city owe their rise to our mismanagement, and that we might as well have had the best part of the tuition-money paid into our treasury, that now goes into private pockets; that there has been a constant disposition to depress the English school in favor of the Latin; and that every means to procure a more equitable treatment has been rendered ineffectual; so that no more hope remains while they continue to have any connection. It is, therefore, that, wishing as much good to the Latinists as their system can honestly procure for them we now demand a separation, and without desiring to injure them; but claiming an equitable partition of our joint stock, we wish to execute the plan they have so long defeated, and afford the public the means of a complete English education.

I am the only one of the original Trustees now living, and I am just stepping into the grave myself. I am afraid that some part of the blame incurred by the Trustees may be laid on me, for having too easily submitted to the deviations from the constitution, and not opposing them with sufficient zeal and earnestness; though indeed my absence in foreign countries at different times for near thirty years, tended much to weaken my influence. To make what amends are yet in my power, I seize this opportunity, the last I may possibly have, of bearing testimony against those deviations. I seem here to be surrounded by the ghosts of my dear departed friends, beckoning and urging me to use the only tongue now left us, in demanding that justice to our grandchildren, that to our children has been denied. And I hope they will not be sent away discontented.

The origin of Latin and Greek schools among the different nations of Europe is known to have been this; that until between three and four hundred years past there were no books in any other language; all the knowledge then contained in books, viz. the theology, the jurisprudence, the physic, the art-military, the politics, the mathematics, and mechanics, the natural and moral philosophy, the logic and rhetoric, the chemistry, the pharmacy, the architecture, and every other branch of science, being in those languages, it was of course necessary to learn them, as the gates through which men must pass to get at that knowledge.

The books then existing were manuscript, and these consequently so dear, that only the few wealthy inclined to learning could afford to purchase them. The common people were not even at the pains of learning to read, because, after taking that pains, they would have nothing to read that they could understand without learning the ancients' languages, nor then, without money to purchase the manuscripts. And so few were the learned readers sixty years after the invention of printing, that it appears by letters still extant between the printers in 1499, that they could not throughout

covering for the head, unless it be the head of a soldier, who has a helmet; but that is evidently not a part of dress for health, but as a protection from the strokes of a weapon.

At what time hats were first introduced we know not, but in the last century they were universally worn throughout Europe. Gradually, however, as the wearing of wigs, and hair nicely dressed prevailed, the putting on of hats was disused by genteel people, lest the curious arrangements of the curls and powdering should be disordered; and umbrellas began to supply their place; yet still our considering the hat as a part of dress continues so far to prevail, that a man of fashion is not thought dressed without having one, or something like one, about him, which he carries under his arm. So that there are a multitude of the politer people in all the courts and capital cities of Europe, who have never, nor their fathers before them, worn a hat otherwise than as a *chapeau bras,* though the utility of such a mode of wearing it is by no means apparent, and it is attended not only with some expense, but with a degree of constant trouble.

The still prevailing custom of having schools for teaching generally our children, in these days, the Latin and Greek languages, I consider therefore, in no other light than as the *chapeau bras* of modern literature,

FRANKLIN'S EDUCATIONAL VIEWS

Thus the time spent in that study might, it seems, be much better employed in the education for such a country as ours; and this was indeed the opinion of most of the original Trustees.

IV

Franklin wrote but little to justify the study of particular subjects, save that to be found in the "Proposals" and the "Constitutions" of the Academy. Mathematics he regarded most highly, though he had at first failed in arithmetic, under Brownell, and mastered it later only by "going through" Cocker's *Arithmetic* by his own efforts; and then he dealt with geometry in the same way, though he never carried this study far. "Arithmetic, accounts, and some of the first principles of geometry . . ." occupied a prominent place in the *Proposals,* coming immediately after "writing a fair hand." In the following essay, the justification for mathematics is found preëminently in its utility but also, as Plato had instructed him, in that ". . . their minds will be improved in reasoning aright . . ." and that all who are found to ". . . have a mind worth cultivating, ought to apply themselves to this study."

FRANKLIN AND THE ACADEMY

On the Usefulness of the Mathematics [41]

From the *Pennsylvania Gazette,* Oct. 30, 1735

Mathematics originally signifies any kind of discipline or learning, but now it is taken for that science, which teaches or contemplates whatever is capable of being numbered or measured. That part of the mathematics, which relates to numbers only, is called arithmetic; and that, which is concerned about measure in general, whether length, breadth, motion, force, etc., is called geometry.

As to the usefulness of arithmetic, it is well known, that no business, commerce, trade, or employment whatsoever, even from the merchant to the shopkeeper, etc., can be managed and carried on without the assistance of numbers; for by these the trader computes the value of all sorts of goods that he dealeth in, does his business with ease and certainty, and informs himself how matters stand at any time with respect to men, money, or merchandise, to profit and loss, whether he goes forward or backward, grows richer or poorer. Neither is this science only useful to the merchant, but is reckoned the *primum mobile* (or first mover) of all mundane

---

[41] SPARKS, JARED, *The Works of Benjamin Franklin,* Vol. II, pp. 66–70, Boston, 1836–1840.

FRANKLIN'S EDUCATIONAL VIEWS

affairs in general, and is useful for all sorts and degrees of men, from the highest to the lowest.

As to the usefulness of geometry, it is as certain that no curious art, or mechanic work, can either be invented, improved, or performed, without its assisting principles.

It is owing to this, that astronomers are put into a way of making their observations, coming at the knowledge of the extent of the heavens, the duration of time, the motions, magnitudes, and distances of the heavenly bodies, their situations, positions, risings, settings, aspects, and eclipses; also the measure of seasons, of years, and of ages.

It is by the assistance of this science, that geographers present to our view at once the magnitude and form of the whole earth, the vast extent of the seas, the divisions of empires, kingdoms, and provinces.

It is by the help of geometry the ingenious mariner is instructed how to guide a ship through the vast ocean, from one part of the earth to another, the nearest and safest way, and in the shortest time.

By help of this science the architects take their just measures for the structure of buildings, as private houses, churches, palaces, ships, fortifications, etc.

By its help engineers conduct all their works, take the

situation and plan of towns, forts, and castles, measure their distances from one another, and carry their measures into places that are only accessible to the eye.

From hence also is deduced that admirable art of drawing sun-dials on any plane howsoever situate, and for any part of the world, to point out the exact time of the day, sun's declination, altitude, amplitude, azimuth, and other astronomical matters.

By geometry the surveyor is directed how to draw a map of any country, to divide his lands, and to lay down and plot any piece of ground, and thereby discover the area in acres, rods, and perches; the gauger is instructed how to find the capacities or solid contents of all kinds of vessels, in barrels, gallons, bushels, etc.; and the measurer is furnished with rules for finding the areas and contents of superficies and solids, and casting up all manner of workmanship. All these, and many more useful arts, too many to be enumerated here, wholly depend upon the aforesaid sciences, viz. arithmetic and geometry.

This science is descended from the infancy of the world, the inventors of which were the first propagators of human kind, as Adam, Noah, Abraham, Moses, and divers others.

There has not been any science so much esteemed and

honored as this of the mathematics, nor with so much industry and vigilance become the care of great men, and labored in by the potentates of the world, viz. emperors, kings, princes, etc.

Mathematical demonstrations are a logic of as much or more use, than that commonly learned at schools, serving to a just formation of the mind, enlarging its capacity, and strengthening it so as to render the same capable of exact reasoning, and discerning truth from falsehood in all occurrences, even subjects not mathematical. For which reason it is said, the Egyptians, Persians, and Lacedæmonians seldom elected any new kings, but such as had some knowledge in the mathematics, imagining those, who had not, men of imperfect judgments, and unfit to rule and govern.

Though Plato's censure, that those who did not understand the 117th proposition of the 13th book of Euclid's Elements, ought not to be ranked amongst rational creatures, was unreasonable and unjust; yet to give a man the character of universal learning, who is destitute of a competent knowledge in the mathematics, is no less so.

The usefulness of some particular parts of the mathematics, in the common affairs of human life, has rendered some knowledge of them very necessary to a great part of mankind, and very convenient to all the rest, that are any way conversant beyond the limits of their own particular callings.

Those whom necessity has obliged to get their bread by manual industry, where some degree of art is required to go along with it, and who have had some insight into these studies, have very often found advantages from them sufficient to reward the pains they were at in acquiring them. And whatever may have been imputed to some other studies, under the notion of insignificancy and loss of time, yet these, I believe, never caused repentance in any, except it was for their remissness in the prosecution of them.

Philosophers do generally affirm that human knowledge to be most excellent, which is conversant amongst the most excellent things. What science then can there be more noble, more excellent, more useful for men, more admirably high and demonstrative, than this of the mathematics?

I shall conclude with what Plato says, in the seventh book of his *Republic,* with regard to the excellence and usefulness of geometry, being to this purpose;

"Dear friend; you see then that mathematics are necessary, because, by the exactness of the method, we get a habit of using our minds to the best advantage. And it is remarkable, that, all men being capable by nature to reason and understand the sciences, the less acute,

FRANKLIN'S EDUCATIONAL VIEWS

by studying this, though useless to them in every other respect, will gain this advantage, that their minds will be improved in reasoning aright; for no study employs it more, nor makes it susceptible of attention so much; and those, who we find have a mind worth cultivating, ought to apply themselves to this study."

CHAPTER V

EDUCATION OF ORPHANS AND NEGROES

Containing "Hints for Consideration Respecting the Orphan Schoolhouse in Philadelphia"; a communication to the *Federal Gazette,* March 25, 1790, "On the Slave Trade"; "An Address to the Public from the Pennsylvania Society for Promoting the Abolition of Slavery, and the Relief of Free Negroes Unlawfully Held in Bondage" (1789); and a "Plan for Improving the Condition of the Free Blacks."

I

THE eighteenth century was an age of many philanthropic, educational ventures. Franklin's philanthropy was, therefore, not unique in all respects. The catholicity of it was, however, unusual. Libraries, schools, hospitals, orphan children and Negroes came, among other things, within its range. His philanthropy with reference to orphans and Negroes was doubtless much influenced by his friends Whitefield and Benezet. But it rested also on a fundamental belief in the equality of all men. The date of the paper, relating to the orphan school in Philadelphia, is unknown but is probably about 1739 or 1740, when he came under the influence of Whitefield whose eloquence induced him on one occasion to give all the money in his pockets, though at first he had resolved to give nothing and then compromised by telling himself he would give only copper money. As one who was "merely an honest man," Franklin had been named one of the trustees of the contributions to erect the building in which Whitefield was to preach. When he became a Trustee of the Academy as well, he had a ". . . good opportunity of negotiating with both, and brought them finally to an agreement . . ." a part of which was that they ". . . maintain a free school for the instruction of poor children. . . ." In 1752, he wrote:

". . . by our opening a Charity School, in which one hundred poor children are taught reading, writing, and arithmetic, with the rudiments of religion, we have gained the general good will of all sorts of people, from whence donations and bequests may be reasonably expected to accrue from time to time. This is our present situation, and we think it a promising one; especially as the reputation of our school increases, the masters

EDUCATION OF ORPHANS AND NEGROES

who in this hot climate are to cultivate our lands? Who are to perform the common labors of our city, and in our families? Must we not then be our own slaves? And is there not more compassion and more favor due to us as Mussulmen, than to these Christian dogs? We have now above fifty thousand slaves in and near Algiers. This number, if not kept up by fresh supplies, will soon diminish, and be gradually annihilated. If we then cease taking and plundering the infidel ships, and making slaves of the seamen and passengers, our lands will become of no value for want of cultivation; the rents of houses in the city will sink one-half; and the revenue of government arising from its share of prizes be totally destroyed! And for what? To gratify the whims of a whimsical sect, who would have us, not only forbear making more slaves, but even manumit those we have.

"But who is to indemnify their masters for the loss? Will the state do it? Is our treasury sufficient? Will the *Erika* do it? Can they do it? Or would they, to do what they think justice to the slaves, do a greater injustice to the owners? And if we set our slaves free, what is to be done with them? Few of them will return to their countries; they know too well the greater hardships they must there be subject to; they will not embrace our holy religion; they will not adopt our manners;

our people will not pollute themselves by intermarrying with them. Must we maintain them as beggars in our streets, or suffer our properties to be the prey of their pillage? For men accustomed to slavery will not work for a livelihood when not compelled. And what is there so pitiable in their present condition? Were they not slaves in their own countries?

"Are not Spain, Portugal, France, and the Italian states governed by despots, who hold all their subjects in slavery, without exception? Even England treats its sailors as slaves; for they are, whenever the government pleases, seized, and confined in ships of war, condemned not only to work, but to fight, for small wages, or a mere subsistence, not better than our slaves are allowed by us. Is their condition then made worse by their falling into our hands? No; they have only exchanged one slavery for another, and I may say a better; for here they are brought into a land where the sun of Islamism gives forth its light, and shines in full splendor, and they have an opportunity of making themselves acquainted with the true doctrine, and thereby saving their immortal souls. Those who remain at home have not that happiness. Sending the slaves home then would be sending them out of light into darkness.

"I repeat the question, what is to be done with them? I have heard it suggested, that they may be planted

EDUCATION OF ORPHANS AND NEGROES

in the wilderness, where there is plenty of land for them to subsist on, and where they may flourish as a free state; but they are, I doubt, too little disposed to labor without compulsion, as well as too ignorant to establish a good government, and the wild Arabs would soon molest and destroy or again enslave them. While serving us, we take care to provide them with everything, and they are treated with humanity. The laborers in their own country are, as I am well informed, worse fed, lodged, and clothed. The condition of most of them is therefore already mended, and requires no further improvement. Here their lives are in safety. They are not liable to be impressed for soldiers, and forced to cut one another's Christian throats, as in the wars of their own countries. If some of the religious mad bigots, who now tease us with their silly petitions, have in a fit of blind zeal freed their slaves, it was not generosity, it was not humanity, that moved them to the action; it was from the conscious burden of a load of sins, and a hope, from the supposed merits of so good a work, to be excused from damnation.

"How grossly are they mistaken to suppose slavery to be disallowed by the Alcoran! Are not the two precepts, to quote no more, 'Masters, treat your slaves with kindness; Slaves, serve your masters with cheerfulness and fidelity,' clear proofs to the contrary? Nor can the plundering of infidels be in that sacred book forbidden, since it is well known from it, that God has given the world, and all that it contains, to his faithful Mussulmen, who are to enjoy it of right as fast as they conquer it. Let us then hear no more of this detestable proposition, the manumission of Christian slaves, the adoption of which would, by depreciating our lands and houses, and thereby depriving so many good citizens of their properties, create universal discontent, and provoke insurrections, to the endangering of government and producing general confusion. I have therefore no doubt, but this wise council will prefer the comfort and happiness of a whole nation of true believers to the whim of a few *Erika,* and dismiss their petition."

The result was, as Martin tells us, that the Divan came to this resolution; "The doctrine, that plundering and enslaving Christians is unjust, is at best problematical; but that it is the interest of this state to continue the practice, is clear; therefore let the petition be rejected."

And it was rejected accordingly.

And since like motives are apt to produce in the minds of men like opinions and resolutions, may we not, Mr. Brown, venture to predict, from this account, that the petitions to the Parliament of England for abolishing the slave-trade, to say nothing of other legislatures, and

EDUCATION OF ORPHANS AND NEGROES

the debates upon them, will have a similar conclusion? I am, Sir, your constant reader and humble servant,

HISTORICUS.[5]

III

Franklin was at all times a friend to the liberation and education of Negroes. While in London he wrote to a number of friends expressing pleasure at seeing the sentiment increase in parts of America in favor of abolition of slavery. One item in his will, £2,172/5 to Richard Bache, was given with the request that he ". . . manumit and set free his Negro man Bob."

To Debby he wrote, June 27, 1760, that he had been chosen as a member of Dr. Bray's Associates. ". . . The paragraph of your letter inserted in the papers, related to the Negro school. I gave it to the gentlemen concerned, as it was a testimony in favor of their pious design. . . ." [6] In another letter, Oct. 4, 1766, he gave advice as to the purchase of real estate in Pennsylvania, to

[5] SPARKS, JARED, The *Works of Benjamin Franklin,* Vol. II, pp. 517–521, Boston, 1836–1840.

[6] SMYTH, A. H., *The Writings of Benjamin Franklin,* Vol. IV, p. 23. (By permission of The Macmillan Company, publishers, New York, 1905.)

a value of £1,000, the profits from which were to be employed in the instruction of Negro children in America. To Anthony Benezet, vigorous opponent of slavery and close friend of Franklin, he wrote that he had prepared a little abstract of information and inserted it in the *London Chronicle,* ". . . with some close remarks on the hypocrisy of this country, which encourages such a detestable commerce by laws for promoting the New Guinea trade; while it piqued itself on its love of virtue, love of liberty, and the equity of its courts, in setting free a single Negro. . . ."[7] A year later he wrote saying he had become acquainted with Granville Sharpe and that they would ". . . act in concert in the affair of slavery. . . ." To Benjamin Rush, six months later, he expressed the hope that ". . . the endeavors of the friends to liberty and humanity will get the better of a practice, that has so long disgraced our nation and religion. . . ."[8]

A few months before he died, he wrote to John Wright: ". . . I wish success to your endeavors for

[7] Aug. 22, 1772. *Ibid.,* Vol. V, pp. 431–432. (By permission of The Macmillan Company, publishers.)
[8] *Ibid.,* Vol. VI, p. 100. (By permission of The Macmillan Company, publishers.)

EDUCATION OF ORPHANS AND NEGROES

obtaining abolition of the slave-trade . . ." and reminded him of the century-old testimony of the Quakers against it and the fact that he had, as early as 1729, printed a book for Ralph Sandyford against slavery and another, a few years later, for Benjamin Lay.[9]

Considering Franklin's disapproval of slavery and his earnest desire to do good, it was but to be expected, when he had at last gained some freedom from exacting public affairs, that he would take a more active part in the abolition movement and seek to promote means of educating Negroes when they had been freed. As the first president of the Abolition Society, Franklin signed a memorial to the House of Representatives of the United States, Feb. 12, 1789, urging the use of all the power vested in them by the Constitution to discourage the inhuman traffic. The memorial caused a wide discussion. Franklin's letter signed "Historicus" was written in answer and parodied a speech given by a Mr. Jackson of Georgia. The following two papers are illustrative of his activities in these respects.

[9] *Ibid.*, Vol. X, p. 61. (By permission of The Macmillan Company, publishers.)

FRANKLIN'S EDUCATIONAL VIEWS

AN ADDRESS TO THE PUBLIC

FROM THE PENNSYLVANIA SOCIETY FOR PROMOTING THE ABOLITION OF SLAVERY, AND THE RELIEF OF FREE NEGROES UNLAWFULLY HELD IN BONDAGE [10]

It is with peculiar satisfaction we assure the friends of humanity, that, in prosecuting the design of our association, our endeavors have proved successful, far beyond our most sanguine expectations.

Encouraged by this success, and by the daily progress of that luminous and benign spirit of liberty, which is diffusing itself throughout the world, and humbly hoping for the continuance of the divine blessing on our labors, we have ventured to make an important addition to our original plan, and do therefore earnestly solicit the support and assistance of all who can feel the tender emotions of sympathy and compassion, or relish the exalted pleasure of beneficence.

Slavery is such an atrocious debasement of human nature, that its very extirpation, if not performed with solicitous care, may sometimes open a source of serious evils.

The unhappy man, who has long been treated as a brute animal, too frequently sinks beneath the common

[10] SPARKS, JARED, *The Works of Benjamin Franklin,* Vol. II, pp. 515–516, Boston, 1836–1840.

EDUCATION OF ORPHANS AND NEGROES

standard of the human species. The galling chains, that bind his body, do also fetter his intellectual faculties, and impair the social affections of his heart. Accustomed to move like a mere machine, by the will of a master, reflection is suspended; he has not the power of choice; and reason and conscience have but little influence over his conduct, because he is chiefly governed by the passion of fear. He is poor and friendless; perhaps worn out by extreme labor, age, and disease.

Under such circumstances, freedom may often prove a misfortune to himself, and prejudicial to society.

Attention to emancipated black people, it is therefore to be hoped, will become a branch of our national police; but, as far as we contribute to promote this emancipation, so far that attention is evidently a serious duty incumbent on us, and which we mean to discharge to the best of our judgment and abilities.

To instruct, to advise, to qualify those, who have been restored to freedom, for the exercise and enjoyment of civil liberty, to promote in them habits of industry, to furnish them with employments suited to their age, sex, talents, and other circumstances, and to procure their children an education calculated for their future situation in life; these are the great outlines of the annexed plan, which we have adopted, and which we conceive will essentially promote the public good, and the happiness of these our hitherto too much neglected fellow-creatures.

A plan so extensive cannot be carried into execution without considerable pecuniary resources, beyond the present ordinary funds of the Society. We hope much from the generosity of enlightened and benevolent freemen, and will gratefully receive any donations or subscriptions for this purpose, which may be made to our treasurer, James Starr, or to James Pemberton, chairman of our committee of correspondence.

Signed, by order of the Society,

B. FRANKLIN, *President*.

Philadelphia, 9th of November, 1789.

PLAN FOR IMPROVING THE CONDITION OF THE FREE BLACKS

The business relative to free blacks shall be transacted by a committee of twenty-four persons, annually elected by ballot, at the meeting of the Society,[11] in the month called April; and, in order to perform the different services with expedition, regularity, and energy, this committee shall resolve itself into the following sub-committees, viz.

I. A Committee of Inspection, who shall superintend

[11] The Society for Promoting the Abolition of Slavery and the Relief of Free Blacks, mentioned in the preceding article.

EDUCATION OF ORPHANS AND NEGROES

the morals, general conduct, and ordinary situation of the free Negroes, and afford them advice and instruction, protection from wrongs, and other friendly offices.

II. A Committee of Guardians, who shall place out children and young people with suitable persons, that they may (during a moderate time of apprenticeship or servitude) learn some trade or other business of subsistence. The committee may effect this partly by a persuasive influence on parents and the persons concerned, and partly by co-operating with the laws, which are, or may be, enacted for this and similar purposes. In forming contracts on these occasions, the committee shall secure to the Society, as far as may be practicable, the right of guardianship over the persons so bound.

III. A Committee of Education, who shall superintend the school instruction of the children and youth of the free blacks. They may either influence them to attend regularly the schools already established in this city, or form others with this view; they shall, in either case, provide, that the pupils may receive such learning as is necessary for their future situation in life, and especially a deep impression of the most important and generally acknowledged moral and religious principles. They shall also procure and preserve a regular record of the marriages, births, and manumissions of all free blacks.

IV. A Committee of Employ, who shall endeavor to

procure constant employment for those free Negroes who are able to work; as the want of this would occasion poverty, idleness, and many vicious habits. This committee will, by sedulous inquiry, be enabled to find common labor for a great number; they will also provide, that such as indicate proper talents may learn various trades, which may be done by prevailing upon them to bind themselves for such a term of years as shall compensate their masters for the expense and trouble of instruction and maintenance. The committee may attempt the institution of some useful and simple manufactures, which require but little skill, and also may assist, in commencing business, such as appear to be qualified for it.

Whenever the committee of inspection shall find persons of any particular description requiring attention, they shall immediately direct them to the committee of whose care they are the proper objects.

In matters of a mixed nature, the committees shall confer, and, if necessary, act in concert. Affairs of great importance shall be referred to the whole committee.

The expense, incurred by the prosecution of this plan, shall be defrayed by a fund, to be formed by donations or subscriptions for these particular purposes, and to be kept separate from the other funds of this Society.

The committee shall make a report of their proceed-

EDUCATION OF ORPHANS AND NEGROES

ings, and of the state of their stock, to the Society, at their quarterly meetings, in the months called April and October.[12]

[12] SPARKS, JARED, *The Works of Benjamin Franklin,* Vol. II, pp. 513–514, Boston, 1836–1840.

INDEX

A

Academie des Sciences, Belles Lettres et des Arts, Lyons, 31
Academies, rise of, 146 *f.*
Academy, at Philadelphia, 116, 137-228, 236
  constitutions of, 182-191
  decline of, 207, 215
  equipment of, 154-156, 188, 204
  "Observations" on, by Franklin, 192-228
  Proposals concerning, 149-181
  salaries at, 144-146, 185, 203 *f.*, 215 *f.*, 218, 222
Academy of Science, Letters and Arts, Padua, 31
Accomplishments, for girls, 130 *ff.*
"Account of the Newly Invented Pennsylvania Fire Places, An," 56
Accounts, 159 *f.*
  to be studied by girls, 131
Activism, as principle of educational method, 37 *ff.*
Adams, ambassador to France, 27
Addison, recommended, 119, 161, 194
"Address to the Public from the Pennsylvania Society for Promoting the Abolition of Slavery, and the Relief of Free Negroes Unlawfully Held in Bondage, An," 236, 248-250
"Advice to a Young Tradesman," 37, 64-67
Agriculture, 176 *f.*
Aims of education, general, 151 *ff.*, 179 *ff.*
  in colleges, 4, 108
  in grammar school, 3
  practical, 101 *ff.*, 116 *ff.*
  religious, 138

INDEX

Albany Convention, 25
Aldus' works, 155
Allen, William, trustee, 117, 183, 193
Alleyne, John, 64
Amboy, N. J., 11
American Academy of Arts and Sciences, Boston, 31
American Philosophical Society, 20, 24, 30, 45, 57-63
Anatomy, study of, 175
Ancestry of Franklin, 1-3
Ancients, use of mathematics among, 232
Antigua, 17
Antiquities, Greek and Roman, 155
Apocrypha, 155
Apollonius, 155
Apprenticeships, Franklin's, 4-5, 8, 10-14
Arbuthnot, on air and aliment, 176
Archimedes, 155
Arithmetic, 130, 159, 173, 183, 187, 228
Armbruster, 18
Art of Thinking, 7
Art of Virtue, The, 84

"Articles of Confederation and Perpetual Union," 27
Astronomy, 159
Autobiography, quoted, 1, 2, 13, 14, 17, 44, 83, 140 *ff.*

B

Bache, Richard, 109, 245
Bache, William, 109, 110
"Bagatelles," 134
Band, The, 44
Banks, Sir Joseph, 23
Bataafsch Genootschap der Proefondervindelijke Wijsbegeerte, Rotterdam, 31
Bathing, 96, 97
Benezet, Anthony, 235, 246
"Benjamin Franklin and the University of North Carolina," 20
Bigelow, John, 35, 43, 54, 62, 94, 131, 133, 142, 144, 239
Blackwell, on rhetoric, 119
Bond, Phineas, trustee, 183
Bonifacius, 7
Books, influence of, on Franklin, 6-7, 150
Boston, Franklin's flight from, 11

INDEX

Braddock's Army, Franklin's assistance to, 25
Bradford, Andrew, 11, 12
Bradford, William, 11
Bray's Association, 245
Brientnall, 15
Brightland's grammar, mentioned, 166
Brockden, 19
Brownell, George, 4, 40, 140
Bunyan, John, 6
Burlington, N. J., 11
Burton, R., 6
Business, prospects, 12 *ff.*
   success, 17-18, 56

C

Cato, 91, 161, 176, 194
"Causes and Cures of Smoking Chimneys, The," 24
Character of Franklin, 9, 18, 35 *f.*
Charity School, 236-238
Charlemagne, 157 *f.*
Charleston, S. C., academy at, 146
   printing business at, 17
Chastity, a virtue, 88, 90
Chew, Mr., trustee, 222
Chronology, 127, 168, 182, 185 *f.*, 202 *f.*
Cicero, quoted, 92
Citizen, Franklin as, 21, 24-30, 36, 56
Citizenship, an objective, 101-102, 168 *ff.*, 179
Classics, in Academy, 173
   chapeau bras. of education, 225-227
   library of, to be available to Academy students, 155 *f.*
   to be taught in translation, 128
Cleanliness, a virtue, 88, 90
Cloyd, D. E., 120
Cocker's *Arithmetic,* 4, 40, 228
Coleman, 15
Coleman, William, trustee, 183
College education, traditional, 4
   criticized by Franklin, 10, 102-109
Collins, 7, 52
Colonial agent, Franklin as, 26
Columella, 176

257

INDEX

Comenius, 37
Commerce, study of, 177
Composition, method of studying, 41-43, 126 f.
Conduct of the Understanding, 7
"Constitutions of the Public Academy, in the City of Philadelphia," 137, 182-191
Continental Congress, Franklin a member of, 26 f.
Copley Gold Medal, awarded Franklin, 30
Courtship and marriage, Franklin's, 13, 16
Coxe, member of Academy committee, 215
Craven Street Gazette, 98
Credit, Franklin on, 64-67
"Crooked Billet," 12
Croxall's *Fables,* 121

D

Dancing, 131
Day of Doom, 6
Deane, Ambassador to France, 27
Debt, on going into, 78 *ff.*

Dechales, 155
Declaration of Independence, Franklin signs, 27
Defoe, Daniel, 6, 102, 130
Deistical tendency, Franklin's, 7 *f.*, 33-35
Denham, Philadelphia merchant, 14 *f.*
Derham's *Physico-Theology, Spectacle de la Nature,* 175
"Description of a New Stove for Burning of Pit Coal and Consuming All Its Smoke," 24
"Dialogue between Franklin and the Gout," 98
Dialogues on Education, 150, 157
Diet, advice on, 98 *ff.*
of pupils, 156
Diophantus, 155
Diplomat, Franklin as, 27-30
"Dissertation on Liberty and Necessity, Pleasure and Pain, A," 14
Dissertations on the English Language, 116
Dogood Letters, 8-10, 103 *ff.*, 130

INDEX

Dogood, Silence (pseudonym), 7, 8, 103, 109, 130, 139
Domestic training, for girls, 132
Dominican Islands, 17
Dove, master in Academy, 205-207
Drake, W. E., 20
Drawing, 129, 158 *f*., 183, 187
Duché, member of Academy committee, 215
Dunlap, printer, 17

E

Easton, Jon., assistant in the Academy, 215 *f*.
Ecclesiastical antipathy, Franklin's 2, 8, 31 *ff*., 132 *f*.
Economy, lessons in, 4, 16, 64-82
Ecton, Northamptonshire, 2
Education, influence of Franklin on, 20, 115 *f*.
  Locke's treatise on, 150, 170 *f*., 177
  of girls, 101, 130-133
  of Negroes, 250 *ff*.
  purpose of, 3, 4, 108, 116 *ff*., 138, 151 *ff*., 179 *ff*.

Electrical experiments, 21-23, 57
Emancipation, of Negro slaves, 239-250
Emulation, encouraged, 173
England, Franklin as envoy to, 26
English Grammar, 120, 122, 160 *ff*., 173, 182, 186, 194 *ff*., 200 *ff*.
English School, Franklin's, 38, 102 *f*., 117-130, 191-228
  proposal to abolish, 216 *ff*.
Essays on Projects, 6
Ethices Elementa, Johnson's, 127
Euclid, 155, 232
Eulogium on Franklin, 45
Eustathius' *Commentaries,* 155
Experiments and Observations on Electricity, published in London and Paris, 22

F

Farnaby's *Rhetoric,* referred to, 164, 199
Father Abraham's Speech, 69-82

INDEX

Federal Gazette, 235, 239
Folger, Peter, 1
Ford, Paul Leicester, 67
France, Franklin as Ambassador to, 27-29, 37
Francis, Tench, trustee, 117, 141, 182 *f.*, 193, 196
Franklin, Abiah (Folger), 1
Franklin and Education, 120
Franklin, Benjamin, sketch of his life, 1-36
Franklin, Deborah (Read), 13, 16 *f.*, 98, 131 *f.*, 245
Franklin, Francis Folger, 17
Franklin, James, printer, 8, 10 *f.*, 18
Franklin, John, 3
Franklin, Josiah, 1, 139
Franklin, Mass., 20
Franklin, Sarah, 17, 131 *f.*
Franklin stove, 56, 95
Franklin, Thomas, 3
Franklin, (Uncle) Benjamin, 2 *ff.*
Franklin, William, 17, 134
"Franklinian theory," 22
French language, study of, 37 *ff.*, 173, 182, 187
  for girls, 132
Frugality, 67, 74 *ff.*, 87 *ff.*, 168

G

Gazette, 184 *f.*, 229
Geography, 127, 129, 159, 168, 182, 185 *f.*, 202
Geometry, 159, 230 *f.*
German, study of, 173, 182, 187
Germans, education of, in Pennsylvania, 112-115
Gilbert, William Kent, 130, 182
Girls' education, 101-102, 130-133, 206 *f.*
Godfrey, 16
Good breeding, to be inculcated, 178 *f.*
Grace, 15
Graevius, 155
Greek, study of, 173, 182, 185
Greenwood's grammar, mentioned, 166
Gronovius, 155
Grotius, works referred to, 155, 171
Guardian, 128

H

Hall, David, 18
Hall, Thomas, assistant in Academy, 215 *f.*

INDEX

Hancock, John, 20
Hardening of body, theory of, 157 f.
Hare, Robert, 191
Harvard College, 109
  honors Franklin, 30
  library assisted, 20
"Health and Long Life, Rules of," 99 f.
Health education, 7, 83, 94-100, 156 f.
Helvicus, 168
Henry the Great of France, 158
Hersan, M., founder of a French school, 153
Hewson, Mary, 101
"Hints for Consideration Respecting the Orphan Schoolhouse in Philadelphia," 235, 237 f.
Historical Collections, R. Burton's, 6
History, 124, 128, 159, 167 ff., 174, 182, 185 f., 202 f.
"History of the College and Academy of Philadelphia . . . ," 130, 182
Homer, recommended, 128
Honors conferred on Franklin, 30-31
Hopkinson, Thomas, trustee, 183
Horace, recommended, 128
House, George, 15
Humility, a virtue, 84 f., 88 ff.
Hutcheson's works referred to, 150, 157, 162, 177, 179, 197
Huygens, 155

I

"Idea of the English School," 101, 103, 117 f., 120-130, 145, 191, 197
Ideas of Beauty and Virtue, 150
Imperial Academy of Sciences, St. Petersburg, 31
Industry, a virtue, 87 ff., 168
  Franklin on, 63-82
Inglis, John, trustee, 183, 223
Italian, studied, 37 ff.

J

Jackson, speech of, on slavery, referred to, 240, 247
Jackson, Richard, 110, 112
Jamaica, 17
Johnson, Samuel, 118 ff., 143 ff.

261

INDEX

Junto, 15, 18, 21, 24 f., 43 f., 50, 56, 95
Justice, a virtue, 87 ff.

K

Keimer, Philadelphia printer, 12, 15
Keith, Governor of Pennsylvania, 12 f.
Kinnersley, Ebenezer, 22 f., 209 f., 212 ff., 222 f.
Kolben, reference to, 113
Königliche Gesellschaft der Wissenschaften, Göttingen, 30

L

Lancaster, Pa., 17 f.
Languages, Franklin a student of, 37 ff.
  too much time on, criticized, 129, 161 ff.
Latin Grammar School education, 3 f., 39, 138
Latin, not proper first step in learning, 39 f.
  study of, 173, 182, 185
Latin School, favored by the trustees, 203-228
  succeeding the vernacular, 38
Law, study of, 171 f.
Lawrence, Thomas, trustee, 183, 223
Lay, Benjamin, 247
Leaping, 157
Lee, Ambassador to France, 27
Leech, Thomas, trustee, 183
Leipzig, Franklin's *Electrical Experiments* published at, 22
Lemery, on foods, 176
"Letter on the Temple of Learning, A," 101, 103-109
Letter writing, 164 ff., 198 f.
Liberal Education, 168
Liberalism, Franklin's, 2, 9, 32, 34, 36, 50 f.
Library, founded at Philadelphia, 19, 193
  of Harvard and at Franklin, Mass., assisted, 20
  to be used by Academy, 155 f.
Life and Correspondence of the Rev. William Smith, 23
"Light-house Tragedy, The," 8
Lipsius, 155

INDEX

Literary interests, Franklin's early, 2 f., 5-10, 14
Locke, John, 7, 150 f., 160 ff., 164 ff., 170 f., 177, 180, 194 f., 199 f.
Logan, James, trustee, 183
Logic, 128, 172, 182, 186, 202 f.
London Chronicle, 246
Lyons, 14

M

Maddox, Joshua, trustee, 183
Manchester (England) Literary and Philosophical Society, 31
Mandeville, 14
"Maritime Observations," 24
Marsigli, Count, interested in school at Bologna, 156
Masters of Academy, duties and qualifications of, 185 ff., 201 f., 204
  tenure, 187
Masters, William, trustee, 183
Mathematics, studied, 40, 129, 156, 183, 187
  value of, 228-234
Mather, Cotton, 7
M'Call, Samuel, Junior, trustee, 183

Mechanics, 125, 129, 156, 177 ff., 183, 187
Medical interests, Franklin's, 95 ff.
Medical Society of London, 31
Medical studies, 175 f.
Memorabilia, 7, 51 f.
Mental discipline, through mathematics, 228
Meredith, 15 f.
Method, in studying composition, 41-43
  of language study, 37-40
  of self-education, 37-100
Middle class education, Academy intended for, 142 ff.
Milton, 119, 150 f., 156, 171, 175 f., 179
Ministry, as career for Franklin, 3 f., 139
Moderation, a virtue, 87 ff.
Modern languages, to be taught, 163 ff., 173, 182, 187, 200
Montfaucon, 168
Montgolfier balloon, Franklin's scientific interest in, 23

INDEX

Moral perfection, aimed at, 83-94
Moral Philosophy, 128
Morals, teaching of, 125, 127, 168 *ff.*
Music, 130, 132
Musschoenbroek, 22

N

Natural History, 176
Natural philosophy, 125, 128, 156, 174 *f.*, 183, 187
Needlework, 130
Negroes, education of, 250-253
  emancipation and provision for, 235, 239-250
New England Courant, 7 *ff.*, 103, 106, 139
New Testament, 155
Newport, R. I., printing business at, 18
Newton, 155
Noetica, Johnson's, 128
Nonconformist tendency, in Franklin family, 2, 7

O

Observations on Liberal Education, in All Its Branches, 150, 181
"Observations Relative to the Intentions of the Original Founders of the Academy," 117, 137, 142, 144, 191-228
Old Bay Psalm Book, 6
On the Education of a Young Gentleman, 150, 172
"On the Slave Trade," 235, 240-245
"On the Usefulness of the Mathematics," 137, 229-234
One-sided education, 134-136
Oratory, 119, 124, 128, 166 *f.*, 169 *f.*, 186, 202
Order, a virtue, 83, 87 *ff.*, 168
  scheme of, 93
Orphans, care and education of, 235-238
Oxford honors Franklin, 30

P

Palmer, London printer, 13
Parker, James, 17
Peace, Franklin on the value of, 27
Pemberton, 14
Penn Charter School, 138, 140
Pennsylvania Hospital, 21, 95

INDEX

Peters, Rev., 117 f., 130, 140, 193, 197, 215, 222
"Petition of the Left Hand, etc., A," 101, 134-136
Philadelphia, Academy at, 137-234
  Franklin's arrival at, 11 f.
  hospital founded at, 21, 96
  improvements at, 21
  library founded at, 19
Philadelphia Zeitung, 17
Philanthropy of Franklin, 19-21, 235-253
Philosophical Society of Edinburgh, 30
Photius, 155
Physical exercise, Franklin's delight in, 5, 14, 55, 96 ff., 156 f.
Pilgrim's Progress, 6
"Plan for Improving the Condition of the Free Blacks," 235, 250-253
"Plan of Moral Education and Self-Examination," 37
Plato, on usefulness of mathematics, 228, 232
Pliny, letter of, on choosing a tutor, referred to, 163 f., 198

Plumstead, William, trustee, 183
Plutarch's *Lives,* 6
Poleni, 155
Political career, Franklin's, 24 ff., 56
Politics, not for women, 132
  study of, 29, 45 ff., 171
Poor Richard's Almanac, 17, 56, 95, 98
Pope, quoted, 51
  recommended, 119, 161, 194
Port Royal, Gentlemen of, 7, 119
Practical affairs, rôle of, in Franklin family, 3 f.
Practical education, stressed, 63-82, 101-136, 158
Premiums, to stimulate pupils, 128 f., 191, 221 f.
Printer, Franklin as master, 15 ff., 56
  Franklin's apprenticeship as, 8, 10
Private school, Franklin at, 4
Pronunciation, to be taught, 166 f., 201 f.
"Proposal for Promoting Useful Knowledge among the British Plantations in

265

INDEX

America, A," 20, 37, 58-62

Proposals Relating to the Education of Youth in Pennsylvania, 137, 141, 147, 149-181, 191, 194, 228

Proverbs, quoted, 92

Prudential wisdom, Franklin's, 64-82

Ptolemy's *Geography* and *Almagest,* 155

Public examinations, 128 *f.*

Publications of Franklin, 7 *ff.*, 14, 17, 22 *ff.*, 47, 56, 58, 64 *ff.*, 84, 95, 99 *ff.*, 103 *ff.*, 116 *ff.*, 120-130, 134 *ff.*, 140 *ff.*, 147 *ff.*, 182, 237 *f.*, 240-245, 248 *ff.*

Puffendorff, *de Officio Hominis & Civis,* and *de Jure Naturali & Gentium,* 171

Purpose, of education, 3, 4, 108, 116 *ff.*, 138, 151 *ff.*, 179 *ff.*

of Franklin's life, 55, 101 *f.*

Pythagoras, *Golden Verses,* 89

R

Ralph, 14
Ratke, 37

Ray's *Wisdom of God in the Creation,* 175

Read, Deborah, 13, 16 *f.*

Reading, 120-123, 162 *f.*

Realistic education, opposition to, 191 *ff.*

Realists, Franklin's agreement with, 38 *ff.*, 147-148, 150-181, 194 *ff.*

Reason, improved by mathematics, 228, 233 *f.*

Rector of Academy, qualifications and duties of, 156, 185 *ff.*, 194, 201 *f.*

salary of, 202

tenure of, 187

Religion, advantage of, 92, 170

"Religion of Nature Delineated," 14

Religious interests, Franklin's, 2, 7, 31-35, 43, 84, 92, 132

Religious purpose, in education, 138 *f.*, 179

Religious training, for girls, 130, 132 *f.*

Republic, Plato's, quoted, 233 *f.*

Resolution, a virtue, 87 *ff.*

Rewards for pupils, 128 *f.*

INDEX

Rhetoric, 119, 124, 128, 170, 183, 185 f., 203

Rhodez, M., quoted, 158

Riding, 157

Rollin's *Belles Lettres,* 150, 151, 153, 162, 167, 174, 180, 196

Rose, Aquila, 11

Royal Academy of History, Madrid, 31

Royal Academy of Sciences, Paris, 31

Royal Medical Society, Paris, 31

Royal Society, Edinburgh, 31

Royal Society honors Franklin, 30

"Rules for a Club Established for Mutual Improvement," 37, 44 f., 47-51

"Rules of Health and Long Life," 37, 95, 99 f.

Running, 157

Rush, Benjamin, 246

S

Salengre, 155

Sanctorius, or perspiration, 176

Sandyford, Ralph, 247

Sayings of Poor Richard, The, 67

Scheme for a New Alphabet and Reformed Mode of Spelling, A, 116

Scientific interests and contributions of Franklin, 18, 20 ff., 45 ff., 55-64

Scientific method, importance of, 54 f.

Scientific societies, Franklin honored by, 30-31
  promoted by Franklin, 56-64

Scientific studies, 125, 128, 156, 174 ff.

Sea-faring life, Franklin's inclination for, 5

Self-education, agencies and methods of, 37-100
  of Franklin, 3, 5-7, 15, 18

Self-rating scheme, Franklin's, 90

Septuagint, 155

"Sermon on Education, A," 118, 130

Shaftesbury, 7, 52

Shakespeare, recommended, 119

Sharpe, Granville, 246

INDEX

Shippen, William, trustee, 183
Shooting, 157
Sidney, Algernon, 161, 194
Silence, a virtue, 87 *ff.*
Simon, M., his criticism quoted by Franklin, 162 *ff.*, 197 *f.*
Sincerity, a virtue, 87 *ff.*
Sketch of Franklin's life, 1-36
Slavery, Franklin on, 239-250
"Slowly Sensible Hygrometer, A," 24
Smith, H. W., 22
Smith, Rev. William, 23, 45, 112, 146
Smyth, A. H., 7, 20, 23, 28, 64, 97, 101, 103, 116, 119, 132, 145, 237, 245
Société Royale de Physique, d'Histoire Naturelle et des Arts d'Orléans, 31
Society for the Encouragement of Arts, Manufactures and Commerce, 30
"Society for Political Enquiries, The," 29
Society for Propagating the Knowledge of God among the Germans, 112
Socratic method, Franklin influenced by, 51-54

Solomon, quoted, 92
Spanish, study of, 37, 39, 173, 182, 187
Sparks, Jared, 46, 67, 100, 117, 136, 192, 229, 238, 245, 248, 253
Spectacle de la Nature, 125
Spectator, 6, 39 *ff.*, 122, 128
Spelling, 120 *f.*, 132
S. P. G., 112 *f.*
Stamp Act, 26
Stiles, Ezra, 33
Strettell, Robert, trustee, 183
Suidas, 155
Swift, recommended, 119
Swimming, 5, 14, 96 *f.*, 157
Syng, Philip, trustee, 183

T

Tacquet, 155
Teachers, to be prepared, 142 *ff.*
Telemachus, recommended, 119, 128
Temperance, a virtue, 84, 86 *ff.*, 96, 98 *ff.*, 168
Tennent's Log College, 146
Theological education, criticized, 107 *f.*, 138 *f.*
  value attached to, 4

INDEX

Theon's *Commentaries,* 155
Thompson, quoted, 92, 154
Tillotson, 160, 194
Tractate of Education, 156, 171, 175, 177, 179
Traditional education, criticized, 102-109
  in New England, 3 *f.*
  persistence of, 137 *f.,* 225-228
Tranquillity, a virtue, 88, 90
Travels of Cyrus, recommended, 119, 128
Treatise on the Passions, A, 150
Trettel, Mr., trustee, 223
Trustees, duty of Academy, 153, 183 *ff.*
  failure of, 192-228
Tryon, 7, 83, 95
Tully's works, 155, 171
Turnbull, Dr. George, 150 *f.,* 156, 162, 165 *f.,* 168 *ff.,* 178 *f.,* 181, 197
Turner, Joseph, trustee, 183

U

Union, The, 44
Universal History, 174

University of North Carolina, Franklin's influence on, 20
University of Pennsylvania, 20
University of St. Andrews, 30
Utilitarian principle, stressed, 40, 55, 63-82, 101-103, 109-136, 158, 229 *ff.*

V

Varro, 176 *f.*
Vernacular school, favored, 38 *ff.,* 102 *f.,* 117-130, 191-228
Vine, The, 44
Virgil, recommended, 128, 177
Virtue, the end of education, 179 *ff.*
Virtues, desired by Franklin, 83-94
  to be inculcated, 168
Vossius, 155

W

Walker, Obadiah, 150, 158, 172
Wallis, 155
War, Franklin's view of, 27
  his experience in, 25
Watts, London printer, 13

INDEX

Way to Health, The, 7
"Way to Wealth, The," 37, 64, 67-82
Wealth, education for, 63-82
   factor in education, 105, 139
Webster, Noah, 116
Weekly Mercury, 11
White, Thomas, trustee, 183
Whitefield, Rev., 32, 235 *f.*
Wigglesworth, 6
William and Mary College, honors Franklin, 30
Williams, Mrs. Linsly R., 67
Willing, Charles, trustee, 183, 223
Willing, master in Academy, 222
Wollaston, 14
Works of Benjamin Franklin, The, ed. by Bigelow, 35, 43, 54, 62, 131, 133, 142, 144, 239
   ed. by Sparks, 46, 67, 100, 117, 136, 192, 229, 238, 245, 248, 253
Wrestling, 157
Wright, John, 246
Writing, 120, 130, 158 *f.*, 164 *ff.*, 183, 187, 198 *f.*, 228
Writings of Benjamin Franklin, The, 7, 20, 23, 28, 64, 97, 101, 103, 116, 119, 132, 145, 237, 245
Wyndham, Sir William, 14, 97

X

Xenophon, 7, 52

Y

Yale College, honors Franklin, 30

Z

Zachary, Lloyd, trustee, 183

LB 575 .F723 1971

Franklin, Benjamin, 1706-
1790.

Educational views of
 Benjamin Franklin

Library
St. Josephs College
Patchogue, N. Y. 11772

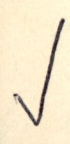